FRAGRANT Magic

modern spells and rituals
to evoke the protective powers
of perfume magic

cassandra eason

quantum

LONDON • NEW YORK • TORONTO • SYDNEY

quantum

An imprint of W. Foulsham & Co. Ltd
The Publishing House, Bennetts Close,
Cippenham, Slough, Berkshire, SL1 5AP, England

ISBN 0–572–02939–X

Copyright © 2004 Cassandra Eason

Printed in Great Britain by Creative Print & Design (Wales), Ebbw Vale.

Contents

	Introduction	4
Chapter 1	Beginning Fragrant Magic	10
Chapter 2	Finding Your Signature Fragrance	24
Chapter 3	Personal Fragrance Magic	33
Chapter 4	Fragrance in the Home and Workplace	49
Chapter 5	Personal Energy Work with Fragrance	62
Chapter 6	Fragrant Dreams	75
Chapter 7	Fragrance and Spiritual Development	88
Chapter 8	Fragrance, Prayer and Angelic Communication	104
Chapter 9	Fragrance, Astrology and Divination	120
Chapter 10	Fragrance and Magic	137
Chapter 11	Healing with Fragrance	149
Chapter 12	Fragrance and Love	160
	Afterword	170
	Fragrant Correspondences	171
	Useful Reading	181
	Useful Contacts	183
	Index	187

Introduction

Fragrance is a very ancient and universal form of magic that enhances the everyday world by increasing our confidence, calming us when we are stressed and enabling us to tap into our own coping strategies. Fragrance can also quickly and effortlessly transport us into beautiful dreams and daytime visions when we need to relax or move away from the frantic world we live in. Anyone who applies a favourite perfume before meeting a lover or going for a job interview is, probably quite unconsciously, tapping into the powers inherent in fragrance to help us to reach for happiness or success if we truly want someone or something enough.

In Ancient Egypt it was believed that fragrances came from the gods, so mortals could become more perfect by absorbing them. In that society, as in countless other cultures, from Native North America to India, the concept existed that each flower, herb or tree has a unique essence or personality that can be absorbed by humans to amplify their own innate talents and charisma.

How fragrance magic works

It is hard not to be lifted physically and emotionally by the scents of a rose garden or a field of lavender, or by pine needles burning in the hearth. Aromas also awaken psychic powers that we all possess but may seldom use. By inhaling scents, whether from growing flowers and herbs or in the form of oils, incense or perfumes, we can connect to a cosmic memory bank – called by the psychotherapist Carl Gustav Jung the collective unconscious – from which we can draw wisdom and power. Through our genetic heritage it may also be possible to link psychically with the experiences and knowledge of people in different times and lands who used similar fragrances or walked in gardens or wind-blown forests filled with similar blossoms. Indeed, fragrances can actually survive thousands of years. When the British Egyptologist Howard Carter opened the tomb of Tutankhamun in the Valley of the Kings on 4 November 1922, he was surprised to find the air still filled with scents that had lasted for 3,000 years, since the young king's burial in around 1322BCE. In the antechamber were two huge wreaths of blue lotus, hibiscus and narcissus, which, although desiccated, were still recognisable.

Gardens have always been very special places. The world began, it is said in some cultures, in a garden, and in the Garden of Eden, in modern-day Iraq, Adam's tree or one of its descendants still grows, albeit a little bedraggled.

What is more, fragrance has the power to heal not only our spirits but also our minds and bodies. Tibetan Buddhists sprinkle patients with – or sometimes immerse them in – water in which flowers have been soaked, and fragrant oils have been a powerful source of healing for centuries and remain so today, whether used in massage, in baths or in an oil burner.

The history of fragrance

The word 'perfume' comes from the Latin phrase *per* meaning 'through' and *fumus* meaning 'smoke'. Indeed, the first scents were burned as incense offerings to the deities in the Middle East 6,000 years ago. Scented oils and fragrant waters for personal as well as ritual purposes became popular by the third millennium BCE in Ancient Egypt, and barrels of fragrant oils and rich incenses were buried in the tombs of the wealthy for their use in the afterlife.

From the most ancient times, fragrant herbs were also hung from ceilings, in huts and palaces alike, to sweeten the air and for magical protection. From about the eleventh century CE in Europe, rushes were scattered on floors in homes, scented with lavender and pennyroyal, herbs that deterred fleas and rats. Flowers and herbs were also worn as garlands for health from Roman times. The children's nursery rhyme 'Ring a Ring o' Roses' recalls the practice of carrying fragrant herbs and flowers to protect against plague epidemics, in this case specifically referring to the Great Plague of London in 1665.

The first modern perfume as we know it was created during the tenth century CE by the Islamic alchemist Avicenna, who distilled oil from rose petals and diluted the essence in water. Though early Christianity discouraged the use of perfumes for personal adornment, monasteries and convents had their own fragrant medicinal herb gardens. Indeed, Maria Prophetissima, often called the mother of alchemy, created a still for healing essential oils as early as the first century CE. Fragrance and health remained closely intertwined, and during the twelfth century the German mystic and herbalist Hildegard von Bingen (1098–1179) made the first healing lavender water to the glory of the Lord, a recipe adopted by young country girls eager to attract earthly lovers.

Eau de cologne, both for medical use and for adornment, was invented in 1732, when the Italian Giovanni Maria Farina made the first *aqua admirabilis* in Cologne in Germany. This was a mixture of neroli, bergamot, lavender and rosemary in grape spirit. The idea travelled to America, where the popular Florida water was a mixture of European eau de cologne with oil of cloves, cassia and lemongrass for added sparkle. No American beauty would set out for a dance without her refreshing water to dab on her wrists, so that she might polka the night through and in the cold light of morning be sufficiently alert to remind her would-be beau of the precise terms and conditions of his euphoric promises of rings and forevers.

During the twentieth century, advances in chemistry allowed the creation of more abstract modern perfumes that released different fragrances during the hours that they remained on the skin. Perhaps most famous is Chanel No. 5, the first completely synthetic mass-market fragrance, produced in 1921.

As we enter the twenty-first century, we are seeing a revival of interest in the aromas of the natural world; some of the older, single floral or woody fragrances such as sandalwood, rose and lavender are regaining popularity, and are often made by small country outlets using indigenous blooms. Bath products, even supermarket brands, are increasingly drawing on woodland and garden and moving away from environmentally unfriendly chemicals. Even kitchen products often contain tea tree oil, mimosa, eucalyptus and orange, so you can weave exotic aromatic daydreams as you wash the dishes.

My own interest in fragrance magic

I have always loved perfume. I remember as a little girl squirrelling away my mother's empty Evening in Paris glass perfume bottles – midnight blue with gold lids – and imagining myself on top of the Eiffel Tower, being fêted and dined. My mother, who was very disappointed with my taciturn father who believed flowers were for funerals, would weave stories about war-time dances at which she was courted by a handsome young Canadian businessman. She told me that Jack, as he was called, wanted to take her back to Ontario as his bride. When the war came, he had to leave hurriedly to join the forces back home. Jack sent my mother tickets through the post to join him, but my grandmother hid the letter away. Years later Jack came back and took my now-married mother to tea in Lewis's department store in the centre of Birmingham. Nine months later, after a long childless marriage, I was born. Who knows whether these were all just stories, but my mother would always dab Evening in Paris behind her ears when we went for tea and iced cakes in Lewis's, and she would get the three-piece band in the restaurant to play 'We'll Meet Again'.

My mother died when I was 19. That Christmas I found an unopened bottle of Evening in Paris and a note saying that my mother had been saving it for me for when I became engaged. I could not bear to use it, but to this day I regret the fact that I threw it away.

Now I live in the countryside, and sage and parsley grow wild in the hedgerows. There are fields of lavender and the wind carries the salt from the sea. Over almost 15 years, as I have written about many different topics, I have been collecting and squirrelling – as I did with those perfume bottles – knowledge about different fragrances, magical herbs, incenses, oils and flowers.

On a recent research trip to Egypt, I visited a perfume workshop, where the manager, Omar, showed me the ancient art of perfume magic. Later, in his family home, he told me some of the perfume lore his father and grandfather had passed down by word of mouth. He also let me smell some of his private family oils and fragrances. Omar said that many of the old families claimed still to know the highly prized secret recipes that the ancient priests of the Temple of the Goddess Hathor at Dendarah would never commit to papyri but only by word of mouth to their trusted successors and apprentices.

The true Egyptian perfumes contain no alcohol and are incredibly expensive, but even a small bottle will last for years. The next day I visited a bazaar, where a guide took me to a traditional incense and spice stall off the tourist track. There, over hibiscus tea, I examined incenses in the forms they had been sold in for millennia and bought some of them to bring home.

About this book

This book is the culmination of research I have carried out over a number of years into oils, incenses and fragrances of all kinds. It has convinced me that they have an important role not only in the everyday world but also in magical ritual for power, success, money, love and healing, as well as in encouraging meditative powers and the altered states of consciousness that make creative dreaming, psychic energy work, astral travel and past-life insights a natural and easy process.

This book draws on traditions from Ancient Egypt and India right through to Native North America and Europe and will enable readers to use their favourite fragrances to create a personal magical and divinatory system. It will also suggest rituals and energy work with essential oils, incenses and smudge sticks.

Using this book

While most of this book can be dipped into in whatever order you wish, I suggest that you read Chapters 1 and 2 first. Chapter 1 outlines the basic materials you will need for fragrance magic and explains how to make your own private fragrant sanctuaries, both indoors and outdoors. Chapter 2 helps you to define your personal signature fragrance, be it an eau de cologne that has sentimental memories or an expensive bottle of perfume that you use at times when you are lacking in confidence or have an important social event, meeting or test. From then on feel free to read the book however you like, choosing those suggestions for practical work that fit in best with your lifestyle and needs.

I have suggested ways you can create your own fragrances from basic easily obtainable ingredients if you wish, but already prepared fragrances and flower waters are just as good and you can empower them to make them your own (see pages 27–31).

On pages 171–80 there is a chart summarising the different uses of many of the various herbs and flowers I have used in the book, as well as any others that are especially potent for fragrance work. Here you can check the healing or magical properties of these plants and the forms in which their fragrance is most commonly found. However, this is not a definitive list and you may wish to add other flowers and herbs. You could photocopy or scan the chart and then scribble in any preferences you have or instances when you have found a flower or fragrant herb to work in an entirely different way.

You will find that you already recognise a number of the ideas I suggest, for they are part of our common ancestral heritage wherever we live. Many flower species, such as lavender and rose, are grown in almost every part of the world, while via the Internet and mail order you can obtain the most exotic oils and herbs at any time of the year. But those plants that grow in your own area are always most potent to work with, as you can see and smell them growing, perhaps drying the petals for yourself or hanging fragrant herbs to form a traditional protective circlet over your door.

If in doubt, trust your instinctive awareness of the scents that are right for you personally as well as magically. For, with fragrances as in all psychic work, we each have our own unique pathway. It leads us above all inwards to self-knowledge and fulfilment, and then outwards to a happier and more successful life.

CHAPTER 1
Beginning Fragrant Magic

Look round your home. On the shelves you will already have a number of fragrances. These may include your favourite perfume, as well as other scents given to you as presents or chosen during long waits in the departure lounges of airports. In the bathroom will be various lotions and bath or shower fragrances, some predicting on the label how you will feel after using them: relaxed, energised, sensual ... (Lavender- and rose-based products tend to be soothing, the more exotic florals or spices, such as jasmine and ylang ylang, may put you in the mood for love, while lemon, bergamot and mint are the get-up-and-goers of the bathroom cabinet.) Shampoos and conditioners may also contain essential oils or herbs: rosemary to give you a mental lift as well as put a shine on your hair, and tea tree to strengthen and heal stressed hair and to deter nits. Even in the kitchen, washing-up liquid and surface cleaners are scented with fragrances formulated to induce optimism about burnt saucepans and trails of curry sauce. As well as the more exotic modern scents, many kitchen and bathroom cleansers contain lemon, lavender and pine, herbs our great-grandmothers used as basic floor cleaners, soaps and polishes – with rather less packaging and rather more elbow grease than I, at least, apply today.

Working with fragrances around your home

As you use different herbal products, become aware of how they affect your mood. Compare the emotional effect of different fragrances used for the same purpose. Experiment with buying new fragrances and note the feelings the aromas evoke in a fragrance journal (see page 15).

Household fragrances are important because they affect the ambience of the home. What is more, they can be used in everyday magic, just as our ancestors used herbs and flowers to magically cleanse and protect themselves and their dwellings. Pine bath foam will wash away personal negativity, a lemon drain cleanser will symbolically prevent family resources draining away, an orange blossom shampoo will give you confidence or help you to negotiate peacefully a tricky patch in a relationship. As you swish a critical relative's tea cup with eucalyptus washing-up liquid, you can clear their hurtful remarks from your mind.

True folk magic uses basic household ingredients and is therefore both very safe and very connected with the real world. So if your fragrant magic comes largely off the shelves of the local supermarket, then you are following a long tradition of people all over the world for whom magic is rooted primarily in the hearth and the home.

Building up your fragrant store cupboard

Many of the basic empowering, healing and protective fragrances are drawn from a relatively small number of flowers and herbs that are now found in many parts of the world. You can therefore begin your collection very easily with the local supermarket, garden centre and healthfood shop. You can add special or more expensive items to your wish list for birthdays and Christmas – and don't forget to treat yourself occasionally as well as treating other people.

You will also need to start collecting storage jars with lids, small stoppered or lidded glass bottles in different colours, dishes, mixing bowls and spoons. Garage sales and cookware remainder shops provide cheap sources of crockery – and you can then throw away dishes that become stained or cracked with constant use. Old dried herb jars can be washed and relabelled as containers for small quantities of unusual herbs. A mortar and pestle, widely available in cookware stores, is useful for magically empowering herbs. Choose a ceramic or marble one rather than wood, which stains.

Keep your magical stores in a cupboard or on a shelf in the kitchen, or in a special magical place in the house. The following are suggestions for building up your basic collection.

✣ **Dried flowers:** These may include dried lavender heads, rose petals and chamomile flowers, all of which can often be obtained from healthfood shops and specialist grocers (look in the herbal tea section of the shop). Sometimes they are on sale in large stores, but be sure they are pure and do not contain fixatives. Store them in dark glass storage jars – you can easily adapt old screw-top coffee jars.

✣ **Dried herbs:** Sage, rosemary, thyme, parsley, basil, peppermint, bay leaves and spices such as cinnamon, ginger and cloves are staples for your store cupboard. In an emergency I have improvised by using a packet of herbal tea bags. If you choose a boxed selection, you can split the individual sachets for an instant supply of dried herbs and flowers. Good independent healthfood shops, old-fashioned groceries and delicatessens often stock such delicacies as loose dried nettles (excellent for protective work) or sugared violets, wonderful for love magic.

✣ **Incense:** Buying incense sticks in different fragrances is a very cheap way of introducing a variety of more unusual perfumes while you are building up your fragrant store. The Body Shop does an excellent floral range very cheaply, and in some places you can buy individual sticks and mix and match. Useful fragrances are carnation, cypress, frankincense, jasmine, lilac, lily, lotus, mimosa, myrrh, sandalwood, vanilla and vetivert. Have some larger incense sticks for outdoor use in such strong fragrances as citronella (also excellent for repelling insects), juniper, pine and vanilla. Buy a little ready-prepared frankincense and myrrh granular incense for special occasions. You can obtain a small metal incense censer and charcoal blocks quite cheaply from New Age and ethnic shops (see Useful Contacts, pages 183–8). If you are using musk or ambergris in any form, choose an artificial kind, as cruelty and destruction are involved in the production of the natural form.

✣ **Essential oils:** The price of these can vary according to the blend; chain-store chemists are a good source of cheaper oils, but make sure they are pure. Begin with lavender and rose otto or rose absolute. These oils can be substituted for almost any other fragrance in magic. Other basics include lemon, orange, rosewood and pine. For a well-stocked store, gradually build up your collection of essential oils to include bergamot, cedarwood, eucalyptus, juniper, lemon balm, lemongrass, lemon verbena, neroli, patchouli and tea tree.

✣ **Carrier oils:** These are used for mixing with and diluting essential oils (which should never be applied neat to the skin as they may cause irritation) and as a medium for other fragrant preparations. Sweet almond is a good all-purpose mixer and diluter. Jojoba, a kind of liquid wax, is very popular in magic and healing work. However, you can also use extra-virgin cold-pressed olive oil or sunflower oil – of the kind that is used for cooking.

✣ **Scented candles:** These useful magical and healing tools are widely available nowadays. Collect them in a variety of fragrances: floral; spicy, such as cinnamon and ginger; the more exotic and ceremonial frankincense, myrrh and sandalwood; and fruity, such as apple, cherry, peach and strawberry (great mood lifters and good for health and love magic). Have a variety of sizes and shapes and store them where they will not get chipped. Candlesticks and holders are also readily available, but look out for unusual ones at antique fairs and garage markets.

✣ **Beeswax candles:** These naturally yellowy honeyed candles can be substituted for those of almost any other fragrance. Look out also for beeswax candles coloured with natural vegetable dyes in green, brown or red. They burn quickly and, being soft, are excellent when you need to press an object into the wax – for instance, coins for prosperity, flowers for love, or crystals for healing. The best source is a country fair or a city market where stallholders come in from the country. Beeswax products are also available via the Internet. Check the list of Useful Contacts on pages 183–8.

✣ **Smudge sticks:** These are tied herb bundles that are burned to release their fragrance. The Native North American sagebrush is easily lit and can be used for many purposes. Cedar and sweetgrass are also available, the latter of which comes as a kind of herbal plait that you can hold or burn in a dish. Smudge sticks are also made in Australia and Europe and may incorporate other herbs, such as rosemary, rosebuds or bay leaves. Keep supplies of large and small smudge sticks – wrapped in cling film or bubble wrap to stop them crumbling – for domestic and personal protective rituals.

✦ **Pot pourri:** Buy two or three small packs of pot pourri, each based on one predominant fragrance, such as lemon, lavender or rose. You can empower these to keep your home harmonious (see pages 27–31). If you have the time and inclination, you can also make your own.

✦ **A container for your signature fragrance (see Chapter 2):** It is a nice idea to keep your special perfume in a stoppered glass bottle or one with a dropper inside the lid. You can then decant it as you need into a small refillable spray to carry with you. Most fragrance manufacturers sell refillable spray bottles. Glass perfume bottles of all kinds are also available from department stores and ethnic shops or via mail order. Look out for ornate ones if you are holidaying in such places as Greece, Turkey, southern Spain, Italy (especially Venice), Egypt or the Middle East. Also keep your eyes open at garage sales and antique fairs. America has a fine tradition of nineteenth-century perfume bottles and you can sometimes pick up good replicas cheaply.

Should you keep magical and culinary herbs separate?

Whether or not you make a distinction between magical and culinary herbs is entirely a matter of choice. As I said at the beginning of this chapter, using household products grounds ritual in reality – no bad thing. What is more, scented candles and pot pourri keep a home psychically harmonious, and I often use half-burnt candles and herbs left over from positive upbeat rituals around the home afterwards rather than throw them away. I do use new ones for each ritual.

However, for practical reasons it may be a good idea to have pots of dried herbs, oils and flower heads as well as basic incense and candles stored ready to use in fragrance work when the need arises. It can be frustrating to find that your flatmate has used all your protective coriander (cilantro) in a stir-fry for her boyfriend or that the last of your extra-virgin olive oil, grown only in one sun-kissed corner of Italy, has been sacrificed to fry your son's bacon sandwiches. Furthermore, if you keep your fragrant ingredients in a special place where you meditate or carry out rituals, over the weeks and months your magical store will both become empowered and will empower the place where it is stored with the individual magical qualities of its contents.

Keeping a fragrance journal

In your fragrance work it is extremely useful to keep a notebook or a computer file to note down blends that you especially like, with exact proportions (it is easy to forget details, especially if, like most of us, you lead a busy life and fit in your fragrance work with a thousand and one other earthly demands). You can also write down also any impressions you receive as you work with different fragrances, whether insights, images or glimpses of past-life worlds. See pages 20–3 and 100–3 for more on past-life work.

Though I have suggested chants, empowerments and healing blessings to strengthen the powers of various fragrances, the best words are always your own, from the heart. Even the most prosaic and business-like among us may create poetry when healing for someone whom we care very much about or speaking to a love yet to be found, and you should write these words down while they are fresh in your mind. Too often I have created a beautiful and inspiring chant and not until later sat down to record it, only to find the words have slipped away.

You can copy notes about your most significant discoveries into an old-fashioned cloth- or leather-bound journal with blank pages, perhaps also pressing precious flowers or herbs that remind you of special occasions. This is a wonderful gift to hand on to future generations, whether your own descendants or the children of people you know. Precious memories and insights do fade, and to record them is to hand on part of your essential self.

Creating a fragrant indoor place

I have carried out rituals in all kinds of places: on the table of a train, in the corner of a café, in sand dunes on a windswept beach and on a corner of my kitchen table – visualising the washing up piled in the sink as a mountain of roses! By inhaling a fragrance and closing your eyes you can create a mystical altar or flower-strewn temple in your mind anywhere.

However, if at all possible, find one special space – large enough to contain a small work table and chair – in which you can concentrate your fragrance work. This could be a curtained-off corner of a room where you relax, an area of your bedroom, a conservatory or even a garden shed (these can be bought quite cheaply from garden and DIY stores). It should be a private place where you will be uninterrupted by the phone, the doorbell or the demands of your family. Women in particular tend to be very good at allowing personal space for others – respecting the privacy of teenagers' bedrooms and partners' workshops – and reluctant to claim it for themselves. Make this personal space your priority.

As well as a table and chair, your fragrant place should also have more comfortable seating or floor cushions. Ideally, choose a space that overlooks the garden or some greenery. If this is impossible, use hanging plants and a shelf of herbs to create a sense of green space. You could also have vases of fresh flowers and bowls of pot pourri in the room. Remember to replace dead flowers, water the plants and change the pot pourri regularly.

No matter how busy you are, try to light a scented candle in your fragrant place at least twice a week, in the evening or early morning, and sit quietly for a few minutes allowing the fragrance to fill you with peace and optimism. If you like, you can also light incense. The list on pages 171–80 details the magical and healing properties of different flowers, fruits, herbs and oils; use it to choose particular incenses, scented candles and oils to suit your mood. As you do your magical work, the power and healing energies of your indoor fragrant place will grow. After a few weeks, you will find that spending just a few minutes in your special fragrant sanctuary, perhaps after a scented bath, will soon restore your equilibrium when you have had a hard day at work or a stressful encounter.

Making a magical altar

Your fragrant indoor place will, as I said, become magical quite naturally. However, if you wish, you can increase its power by making your work table into a more formal magical altar. An altar is simply a sacred space and acts as a focus for your magical activities. At the centre you can keep your signature fragrance, while the four quarters of the altar should be aligned to the main direction points. The energies of the directions will further enhance the power of your magical work. You can use a compass to align your altar, or you can work out the approximate directions in relation to local landmarks.

Each direction is associated with one of the four elements, Earth, Air, Fire and Water. These elements were first identified in Ancient Greek times. They were believed to be the building blocks of all existence and present in every person in varying proportions. In magic it is said that by combining the energies of the four elements in ritual it is possible to create a fifth element that makes anything possible. In modern times, the psychotherapist Carl Gustav Jung also subscribed to the concept of the four elements, identifying them as important human psychological and psychic factors.

Earth
Using one of the Earth fragrances listed below, set a bowl of pot pourri or dried petals or herbs in the northern quarter of the altar to symbolise the strength of Earth empowering your indoor fragrant place and your magical and healing work.

Qualities: Stability, common sense, practical abilities, caretaking of the earth, protection, upholding of tradition, love of beauty, patience and perseverance, generosity, acceptance of others, nurturing powers and permanence.

Controls: Abundance and prosperity, fertility, finance, law and order, institutions, authority, motherhood, the physical body, food, home and family, animals, the land, agriculture, horticulture, environmentalism, womb and tomb.

Earth places and forces: Megaliths, stone circles, groves, forests, homes, gardens, temples, crypts, caves, rocks, mountains, castles and castle walls, trees, earthquakes.

Earth fragrances: Cypress, fern, geranium, heather, hibiscus, honeysuckle, mimosa, oakmoss, patchouli, sagebrush, sweetgrass, vervain and vetivert.

Air
Using one of the Air fragrances listed below, place incense sticks or cones in the eastern quarter of the altar to symbolise the energies of Air empowering your indoor fragrant place.

Qualities: Logic, clear focus, an enquiring and analytical mind, the ability to communicate clearly, concentration, versatility, movement, adaptability, strong self-identity, the quest for truth, commercial and technological acumen, healing powers.

Controls: New beginnings, change, health and healing, teaching, travel, house or career moves, knowledge, examinations, the media, science, ideas, ideals, money-spinning.

Air places and forces: Mountain tops, towers, steeples and spires, the sky, pyramids, open plains, tall buildings, balconies, roof gardens, tree tops, winds of all kinds (including whirlwinds and tornadoes), thunder.

Air fragrances: Acacia, almond, anise, benzoin, bergamot, dill, fennel, lavender, lemongrass, lemon verbena, lily of the valley, marjoram, papyrus flower, peppermint, sage.

Fire

Using one of the Fire fragrances listed below, set scented candles in the southern quarter of the altar to symbolise the energies of Fire empowering your indoor fragrant place.

Qualities: Fertility in all aspects of life, creativity, light-bringing, power, self-esteem and confidence, passion, joy, initiative, transformation, courage.

Controls: Ambition, achievement, illumination, inspiration, all creative and artistic ventures (poetry, art, sculpture, writing, music and dance), religion and spirituality, psychic powers, innovation, sexuality. It is also potent for destruction of what is no longer needed and for protection of all kinds.

Fire places and forces: Hearths, deserts, volcanoes, fires of all kinds (including sacred festival fires, hilltop beacons, bonfires and forest fires), lightning, the sun and solar eclipses.

Fire fragrances: Allspice, angelica, basil, bay, carnation, cedarwood, chamomile, cinnamon, cloves, copal, dragon's blood, frankincense, heliotrope, juniper, lime, marigold, nutmeg, orange, rosemary, tangerine.

Water

In the western quarter of the altar place a bowl filled with cologne, rose or lavender water; rose petals in water; or water scented with oils in one of the Water fragrances listed below. This will symbolise the energies of Water empowering your indoor fragrant place.

Qualities: empathy, inner harmony, peacemaking, unconscious wisdom, ability to merge and interconnect with nature and with others, self-love, reconciliation, the cycle of the seasons, the moon, intuition, fluidity.

Controls: Love, relationships, friendship, dreams, purification of negativity, perfume magic, moon magic, travel by sea.

Water places: The ocean, rivers, lakes, pools, streams, sacred wells, waterfalls, marshland, floods and flood plains.

Water fragrances: Apple blossom, apricot, coconut, eucalyptus, feverfew, heather, hyacinth, jasmine, lemon, lilac, lily, melissa (lemon balm), myrrh, orchid, passionflower, peach, strawberry, sweet pea, thyme, valerian, vanilla, violet.

The simplest way to make use of the energy of the directions is to face each one in turn, beginning in the North, and ask aloud for its elemental powers to enter a fragrance, an oil or even a bath product you are going to use before a special date or an important day at work. For more on ways to work with the directions in fragrance magic, see pages 41–3.

Creating a fragrant outdoor place

On sunny days, sitting in the open air among natural fragrances or tending growing plants is a soothing antidote to the pace of modern living. Some of my most magical outdoor times are early mornings after rain and summer evenings as the last insects buzz around lavender and roses.

Your outdoor fragrant place could be a scented area in your garden, tubs on a patio or balcony, or even a rarely visited spot in a nearby park or botanical garden that you can call your own. It should include herbs such as lavender, rosemary and chamomile, which are particularly fragrant and will grow almost anywhere. They also have many uses in magic and healing. Be aware that some herbs, such as vetivert, are more fragrant as oils, incense and scented candles and so will not add perfume to your outdoor place. Other herbs give off an aroma that some people find unpleasant. Valerian, for instance, has been described as nauseating – though I love the smell of the fresh herb. Smell pot herbs in a garden centre before buying and if you don't like the fragrance, substitute a different herb. Chamomile, for instance, resembles valerian in its appearance but smells gently sweet. If you're not sure about the smell of a particular herb, crush its leaves or flowers; its aroma will become stronger – and generally more pleasing. Alternatively, smell the herb after rain.

If possible, your outdoor fragrant place should also include roses. If space is limited, use tiny scented pot roses. The rose has been sacred to love goddesses in many times and cultures, including the Egyptian Hathor and the Graeco-Roman Venus (see pages 161–4 for more on roses). It is also a symbol of gentleness and healing, and can help in overcoming all kinds of abuse, sorrow and trauma.

Another good addition to your fragrant outdoor place is a stone with a flat top. Place it in the centre and use it as a work table or altar for your rituals and empowerments. If your place is in the park, you could take a special cloth to place on the grass.

Try to work in your outdoor fragrant place in different seasons, warmly wrapped up if need be. The damp autumn leaves and cider fragrance of crushed apples; the dank chill of winter, its winds carrying the tang of pine needles and bonfires of fragrant wood; the freshness of spring violets and the first cherry blossom; and the heady blooms of summer all create entirely different moods. With the help of a good book or a friendly local garden centre, you can choose fragrant plants for different times of the year and bring your favourite seasonal offerings to the indoor altar around the calendar.

Using fragrance as a catalyst for your own psychic powers

Of all our psychic senses, clairsentience – gaining impressions through psychic means – is the most spontaneous. We may, for instance, feel instinctively that a house is unfriendly or dark no matter how brightly painted the rooms are or how sunny the day. Questioning will usually reveal that an unhappy event occurred there, the impression of which has become imprinted in the atmosphere. On the other hand, we may pick up happy impressions of people who have lived and loved and perhaps spent their entire life in a place, whether as Lady of the Manor or as a serving maid.

Smelling an actual fragrance in the garden or rooms of an old building will readily trigger this clairsentient ability to experience images and scenes from the past. In an aromatic herb garden in a ruined abbey near Linkoping, in central Sweden, my friend Susanne and I independently had visions of an abbess in the garden scolding two young novices for skipping out of church. One of the girls was taken away over the seas by invaders, who killed the Abbess and kidnapped or raped and killed the other nuns. The other girl hid behind the altar and in time revived the abbey and became Abbess herself. Afterwards Susanne read the abbey's history on a plaque on the wall and, translating, told me that we had in fact been standing in the Abbess's garden. Further research revealed that the abbey had been raided in the eleventh century and most of the girls taken away across the sea or killed.

All this we had seen in our minds, triggered by the scents of the garden. Neither of us had been to the place before and we had discovered it quite by chance.

Using fragrances for clairsentience

Certain fragrances that possess a long tradition in different ages and cultures offer almost instant access to the collective folk memory. If you work with these fragrances repeatedly, your psychic channels will become sensitised to picking up information by this route. Once activated, your clairsentient powers will enable you to tune in easily to past impressions around any old building or sacred site, especially if one of the timeless fragrances is present there, like a key unlocking a door.

Even if you are experienced psychically, you may find the following method helpful to fine-tune your clairsentient abilities before you visit an old house or garden. Before you start you will need to buy a variety of herbs, fruits or flowers from the following list – or alternatively visit a garden where they may be growing. These herbs, flowers and fruit fragrances are especially evocative: basil, bayleaf, eau de cologne, eucalyptus, honeysuckle, jasmine, lavender, lemon, lemon verbena, lime, mimosa, mint, orange, pine, rose, sage and thyme. If any of these plants do not grow in your region, you can burn them as candles, incenses or oils in your indoor fragrant place. Alternatively, substitute strong-smelling plants that are indigenous to the area in which you live.

Once you have made your collection, choose up to three of the fragrant plants to work with in this session. Taking each herb, flower or fruit in turn, close your eyes and inhale its fragrance. As you do so, concentrate not so much on what you see and hear as what you feel – for instance, peace, joy or sudden knowledge about a place or time where the fragrance had significance. You may also hear sounds, voices or music. Pay attention to what they evoke. Afterwards, make notes in your fragrance journal of your impressions and any events that are linked in your mind with the scent – weddings, battles, monks singing Vespers in a chapel ... Also pay attention to any dreams that you have subsequently: they may contain clairsentient information.

Here are some more ideas for honing your clairsentient powers.

✣ Try working with other strong smells, for example spices such as cinnamon, garlic and ginger; baking bread; old-fashioned lavender polish and beeswax candles.

✣ Visit the sea or a salt lake or marsh, close your eyes and taste the tang in the air. Note any strong emotions or scenes it evokes.

✣ If you are going on holiday abroad, the week before you travel focus on oils or incenses of aromatic plants that grow in your holiday destination. During your stay, visit any traditional flower markets or herb shops or stalls. Close your eyes and you may instantaneously link into the memories of the culture you are visiting. As you absorb the fragrance of the exotic flowers and fruits growing around you, these impressions may grow stronger.

Testing your clairsentient powers

Clairsentience isn't something that you have to prove to yourself or anybody else; however, the following is a fun exercise if you want to find out how your powers of intuition are developing.

When you are in an unfamiliar area, choose intuitively an old castle, monastery, abbey, temple or ancient sacred site to visit. Find a quiet corner in your chosen place – for instance a seat in the herb or rose garden, or some old stones that were once part of a wall near fragrant bushes. Sit down and pay attention to your impressions. Not only will you obtain a rich sense of the place and its history but you may also recognise it instinctively from your clairsentient experiments or from dreams resulting from your clairsentient work.

Now do some research. Find history books and guidebooks, talk to local people and look on the internet. See what you can find out about the place you have visited. You may find that you have sensed events that actually took place.

CHAPTER 2
Finding Your Signature Fragrance

We all have a special signature fragrance, one that when we wear it makes us feel special, confident, harmonious and at ease even in unfamiliar or challenging situations. We may have been wearing it the night we met our first love, have bought it with our first wage packet or been given it for a birthday present or as a spontaneous gift of love. It may be an expensive perfume, such as Chanel No. 5 – one that you buy only at airports in the flush of holiday extravagance – or it may be something more homely but equally potent, for example Yardley's English Rose, recalling sunny days as a child floating rose petals in water, when anything seemed possible. A signature fragrance may evoke memories of perfect happiness or beautiful places, of the heady scent of orange trees in bloom or mimosa trees in moonlight, their star-like white blossoms fragrant after rain.

However, you may not yet have found your signature fragrance. You may use perfumes that you like but which never feel part of you. Or you may have outgrown a familiar perfume. Motherhood and the menopause may bring hormonal changes that make a scent worn for years seem suddenly slightly off note, while divorce, remarriage, children leaving home, promotion, moving to a new area, redundancy, a new career later in life or retirement may necessitate a new fragrance for a changed life style.

Why you need a signature fragrance

A signature perfume is a statement of what we are and what we have the potential to be. What is more, as we wear it over the years, it becomes empowered by our own unique qualities and strengths and by our memories of the happy and successful occasions on which we were wearing it. So when you are feeling low or have hit a crisis, applying your special scent can instantly fill you with optimism and activate your inner power to overcome any obstacle.

Let me give you an example from my own life. My signature perfume is Arpège by Lanvin. It was first introduced to me when I was a young teacher, struggling to live in London on relatively low wages. The headteacher of the school where I worked, Margaret, would spray Arpège on my wrists and brow when I was tired, stressed or had a headache. I instantly relaxed and became confident and energetic once more. But more than that the perfume represented for me a better life, as Margaret came from a working-class background similar to my own but had struggled her way to success by hard graft and willpower.

When I left teaching to have a baby, Margaret bought me a bottle of Arpège to take into hospital. I sprayed it on my pillow during a long, painful labour. In the following days, I struggled with the demands of new motherhood that seemed to engulf my identity and leave me feeling totally inadequate and scared, something I had not anticipated, since I thought I knew all there was to know about children! The fragrance was a reminder that I did still exist in spite of my exhaustion and a baby who, no matter what I did, yelled his head off while my impatient husband insisted that mothers were supposed to know what to do automatically.

I bought my own Arpège for the first time the day after my husband left me and the baby to move in with a glamorous and childless older woman. It was an act of defiance on my way to a job interview. Though I could not afford such an expensive perfume when I was worrying about how to keep a roof over our heads, I dowsed myself in fragrance and got the post I needed.

Identifying your signature fragrance

One of the best places to discover your signature fragrance is an old-fashioned perfume shop where there is a wide range of fragrances and experienced staff who will help you to isolate three or four perfumes from which to make a final choice. If there isn't a shop like this in your area, visit a large department store, stopping at each of the different perfume counters and allowing your instincts to draw you to particular fragrances. If you are uncertain which to try, ask if there are any small sample bottles you can take home.

When you have three or four favourite fragrances, to avoid mingling apply them to pulse points as far away from each other as possible, for example separate wrists and your throat. Ask if there are bottles with stoppers or droppers for testing rather than sprays so that you can drop the perfume onto a small area of skin. You should always try perfumes on because they smell very different on the skin than they do in the bottle. Furthermore, each person's individual body chemistry will interact with a fragrance differently, so a perfume that smells wonderful on a friend may be totally wrong for you. (For this reason using strips of blotting paper, a traditional method of trying perfumes, is not very helpful in finding your signature fragrance.)

After initially smelling the fragrance on your wrists or throat, you should wait an hour or so and then smell it again, as it will have changed slightly. Then smell it a third time after three or four hours – there will have been yet another change as different essences within the fragrance have come to the fore. These subtle changes are called the 'notes' of a perfume. If you are still uncertain, go back to the store and try the perfume again on another day.

However, for many people the right fragrance is an instant and lasting love affair, and once they have smelled it and applied it there really is no question of needing to try anything else.

Tips for choosing a fragrance

✢ Go perfume shopping during the late afternoon or early evening as your sense of smell is at its most discriminating around dusk.

✢ If you are uncertain which perfume to try, hold the fingers of your power hand (the one you write with), with the palm curved slightly downwards, over the various bottles. Some people believe that there are psychic energy centres in the centre of our palms, linked to the heart chakra (see pages 66–7). By tapping this source of power it is possible that you will be drawn intuitively towards the perfume that is right for you. A tingling sensation over a bottle indicates that you are connecting on an instinctive level with that particular fragrance and should try it on your wrist.

✢ The smell of coffee beans takes away the aroma of perfume, so if you are feeling overwhelmed by fragrance, stop for a cup of coffee.

Decaffeinated is just as good. Alternatively, carry a resealable sachet of coffee beans with you and sniff them between perfumes.

If your signature perfume turns out to be very expensive, don't forget that bottles come in different sizes and you can always buy a more dilute form, such as eau de cologne. In leaner times I have resorted to the deodorant or even the soap version of a more expensive fragrance. Remember that good perfumes do last all day and you need far smaller quantities than you do of cheaper scents, even in warm weather. We sometimes hesitate to spend money on ourselves when we would happily buy a child the latest computer game or treat friends or family to a meal in a pizza house costing the equivalent of a modest bottle of perfume.

Wearing your signature fragrance

Your fragrance should be the first thing you put on in the morning, after your bath or shower, applying it to slightly damp skin. You might like to use a matching soap and deodorant or find a delicate aroma that harmonises.

If you are using a spray bottle, hold it about 20 cm/8 in from your body, as this will create a fine mist for best effect. Otherwise you can focus on the pulse points, which include the wrists, neck, collarbone, back of the knees and ankles. Many glass bottles have a dropper or a stopper that can be used to apply perfume.

Carry a small bottle of the fragrance around with you in your handbag so that you can top yourself up mentally with a drop or two of confidence before a challenging meeting, important interview or hot date.

Empowering your fragrance

Though I have spoken of discovering your signature fragrance, if you go for a commercial perfume, no matter how expensive, you can guarantee that thousands of other people will also be using it. Indeed, it is said that after Marilyn Monroe announced that she wore nothing but Chanel No. 5 in bed, a million women rushed out to buy the perfume.

Nevertheless, I do believe that perfume becomes unique, both because it combines in a completely unique way with your natural body chemicals and because as you use it over the years its history intertwines with peak moments in your own life and with crises when you somehow survived and bounced back against the odds. In order to make your perfume particularly potent and personal, however, there are simple rituals that you can use to empower each new bottle. These can be especially helpful if you have changed to a new signature fragrance or adopted one for the first time. Of course, if you're half way through a bottle of perfume as you read this book, there's no reason why you shouldn't empower that, making it a storehouse of all your personal potential and a reminder of everything you have achieved and will attain in the future.

Candlelight empowerment ritual

Carry out this ritual once a week.

What you need: A small beeswax candle or a candle scented with sandlewood or rose, a suitable holder.

✢ Light the candle and place it on the altar.

✢ Sitting in candlelight, hold the bottle between your hands so that the light shines on it and your personal energies, transmitted through your palms, can strengthen it.

✢ Name anything good that has happened during the week or, if it has been a challenging time, list all your strengths and good qualities and picture them entering the fragrance as tiny beams of light.

✢ When you have finished, blow out the candle and picture the candlelight entering the fragrance and also surrounding you.

✢ Leave the bottle on the table or altar in your indoor fragrant place.

Full moon empowerment ritual

This ritual should be carried out on the night of the full moon, at dusk, as the moon is rising. If the weather is not conducive to working outdoors, you can work in your indoor fragrant place and light a circle of silver candles around the perfume bottle.

What you need: Tiny silver-coloured items (for example coins, earrings, rings, Christmas baubles, silver bells).

✣ Set the bottle in your outdoor fragrant place, somewhere where the full moon will shine on it. Surround it with the silver items (silver is a colour sacred to the moon).

✣ Leave the bottle in place until you go to bed and then return it to a central position on the table or altar in your indoor fragrant place, still surrounded by the silver items. (You can remove these the following evening.)

White flower empowerment ritual

Carry out this ritual at any time when you sense you will need extra power.

What you need: Fresh fragrant white flowers or white silk flowers perfumed with a few drops of rose or lavender water.

✣ At dusk encircle the perfume bottle with the flowers. Leave it on your work table or altar overnight.

✣ In the morning, after your bath or shower, anoint the centre of your brow with a single drop of the fragrance, stating the power you need. Take one of the flowers with you as you for courage as you embark upon your day.

Earth, Air, Fire and Water empowerment

This ritual is more complex than the others. It draws upon the powers of the four elements to link your own good qualities with natural forces and so psychologically amplify your own inner strengths. Work this ritual as dusk is falling. You can repeat it at any time when you need special strength, if necessary changing the words of the chants to include those elemental places and qualities that most closely fit your needs.

What you need: Scented nightlights or small scented candles in pink or purple (both colours of spiritual work); suitable holders; dried herbs, flower petals or pot pourri in your favourite Earth fragrance (see page 17); an incense stick in an Air fragrance (see page 18); a scented candle in a fire fragrance (see page 18); some eau de cologne or water instilled with petals of a Water fragrance (see page 19), a small fragrance spray bottle.

✣ Have a fragrant bath or shower and slip into something comfortable.

✣ Go to your indoor fragrant place and light the nightlights or candles. Place your bottle of fragrance at the centre of your work table or altar.

✣ Sit for a while in the candlelight thinking about what Earth, Air, Fire and Water mean to you.

✣ Begin by empowering your fragrance with the energy of Earth. Scatter the herbs, petals or pot pourri in three clockwise circles around the perfume, moving the circles from the centre outwards. As you scatter, say softly three times:

> *Earth power, at this hour, power of rock and tree and cave,*
> *bring to me strength and stability.*

✣ Next, empower your fragrance with the energy of Air. Light the incense stick and circle the bottle with it clockwise three times, again moving the circles from the centre outwards, saying softly:

> *Air power, at this hour, power of mountain, wind and plain,*
> *bring to me focus and identity.*

Then write your name as though it were a signature in the air above the bottle.

✣ Next, empower your fragrance with the energy of Fire. Light the scented candle and pass it carefully over the perfume bottle, being careful not to drip wax on it. Make three clockwise circles, moving outwards from the bottle. As you circle, say:

> *Fire power, at this hour, power of lightning, sun and fire, give*
> *to me courage in life and clarity.*

✣ Finally, empower your fragrance with the energy of Water. Sprinkle three circles of eau de cologne or fragranced water clockwise around the bottle, once again moving outwards from the bottle. As you do so, say:

> *Water power, at this hour, rivers rushing to the sea, bring to me*
> *self-love and harmony.*

✣ Now fill the small fragrance spray from the empowered bottle. Know that when you hold it between your hands, just before an important meeting for example, you will be able to visualise the elemental energies entering the fragrance and giving it power.

Enchanting your fragrance

Enchantment is an age old ritual practised by wise women through the ages. Even in ordinary homes, our foremothers taught their daughters how to make a home-made scent attract love, health or happiness, or bring work to a home where there was financial hardship.

You can use enchantment as an alternative to an elemental empowerment (such as those above) when you first obtain your bottle of perfume. This will be equally effective. You can also use enchantment in addition to empowerment, enchanting your fragrance for even more potency at times of change or when you need a great deal of impetus to take a leap forward mentally or emotionally. You can enchant either generally or for a specific purpose, for example to draw a new love or deepen an existing friendship, to attract success or promotion at work, to ensure good fortune in a new business venture, to help you pass an examination or test, to bring prosperity or better health, to ensure that a family gathering is harmonious, or even to alleviate fear before flying.

You can enchant other fragrances, but your signature fragrance will always be the most powerful for personal use.

A basic enchantment

What you need: (If you are enchanting a small amount of fragrance for a specific purpose) a bowl to contain your fragrance, an eye-dropper, a small fragrance spray bottle.

✢ Take your bottle of fragrance to the table or altar in your indoor fragrant place. If you are not enchanting the whole bottle, pour a little of the fragrance into the bowl.

✢ Now practise the hand movement that you will need to make for this enchantment. Hold your hands horizontally at waist height, with your elbows bent, your palms facing downwards and your fingers close together pointing straight ahead. Move your left hand anticlockwise and, at the same time, your right hand clockwise in a slow steady rhythm.

✦ Once you are adept at this movement, hold your hands a few centimetres above the bottle or bowl of fragrance and as you move them in unison begin a spontaneous chant naming either the purpose of the empowerment and the blessings or strengths you need or (if your enchantment is in place of an empowerment) naming all your unique qualities. For example, if you were meeting your prospective in-laws for the first time, you might say something like:

> *Bring harmony and unity. May Dawn and John welcome me into their family for what I am, as I am, and not what they wish me to be.*

✦ Repeat the chant continuously until you sense that the fragrance is empowered with blessings and light. You may detect a slight glow around it either in your mind's eye or externally.

✦ If the enchantment is for a specific purpose, using the eye-dropper transfer some of the perfume from the bowl into your small spray bottle to carry with you to use before the named encounter or task. As you apply the fragrance before this event, repeat the chant in your head or aloud over the bottle.

CHAPTER 3
Personal Fragrance Magic

In this chapter we will be working with traditional methods of personal enhancement using herb and flower waters and oils. We will be making magical fragrances that you can give as gifts to family and friends, and we will be developing a repertoire of favourite recipes, which you can record in your fragrance journal to hand on to future generations.

Throughout the ages the women of the household made flower waters and colognes, bath salts and infused floral oils to enhance their natural beauty and to attract love and good fortune. In many families a recipe for love, fertility or happiness was handed on through the generations, often with a secret ingredient or charm that made it unique. In the modern busy world much folk wisdom has been lost from family life, and we may no longer have ready access to the herbs and flowers that were once freely gathered from hedgerows or grown in cottage gardens.

However, many of these old preparations are quick and easy to make, and can form a focus for our own needs and dreams as we mix the ingredients. If time is at a premium, it is also quite acceptable to buy natural herbal products and empower or enchant them with one of the rituals I suggest (see pages 27–32).

Though your signature perfume is your single most important magical fragrance, more homely scents can bring health, happiness, harmony, love and prosperity to your everyday world. You can use a specific infused oil, floral water or cologne in addition to your signature fragrance or as a substitute for it. If a magical need is one that will take several days or weeks to fulfil, you might like to keep your signature fragrance for special occasions or bursts of power.

The flowers or herbs you choose will influence the particular powers with which your mixture is infused, so work with plants appropriate to your purpose, for example rose for love, lilac for happiness, and rosemary for concentration, good fortune and passion. You can make the precise combination of qualities you seek by adjusting the proportions of the herbs. For example, you might add more rosemary to a rosemary and rose water in order to attract passionate rather than gentle romantic love.

Making your own magical fragrances

Because I am not a craft-orientated person and my time tends to be limited, my methods are very simple. If you would like to make more complex mixes, there are several books that tell you how to do it (see page 181). The secret, however, is not in how long it takes to create your potion but in the positive energies with which you endow it.

Equipment

You will need to collect containers for your fragrances. Large and small screw-top medicine bottles are good, both dark and clear, as are storage jars with airtight lids. Old bath foam and essential oil bottles are also useful, and the latter often have dropper tops. Make sure you wash your containers thoroughly before you reuse them, especially if they have contained essential oils.

You will also need plastic or glass filter funnels for straining herbs and petals. You can find these in cookware stores as well as pharmacists. For straining infused oils you can use old-fashioned muslin or cheesecloth. Eye-droppers are useful for transferring small quantities of oils and fragrances, and you will need sticky labels so you can identify the fragrances you have made, their purpose and the date they were prepared.

Ingredients

You can obtain flower petals and heads, such as rose and lavender, from plants grown in the garden. You can buy flowers specifically for your fragrant magic from garden centres and grow them in pots. You can often buy fresh herbs in supermarkets.

For some recipes you will need pure 100 per cent proof vodka (a cheap one is fine) and for others a good quality cold-pressed oil such as sweet almond, olive or jojoba.

Timings

Traditionally, the preparation of infused oils is started at the time of the crescent moon. Beginning when the lunar energies are gently increasing gives oils a power that grows as the fragrance slowly seeps into the oil, even if the preparation time lasts into a second month.

Colognes and oil-based perfumes that require a shorter preparation should be made when the moon is in an appropriate phase for your needs. The time of the waxing moon, which lasts approximately 14 days from the crescent to the night of the full moon, can be used for creating mixtures for bringing gradual increase. The full moon is ideal for making preparations that will introduce change and fresh energies into your life. Finally, the time of the waning moon, from the day after the full moon to the end of the lunar cycle (when the moon disappears from the sky), is useful for preparing fragrances to use in removing what is unwanted, for example a negative self-image, a destructive relationship or a bad habit. Diaries, calendars and the weather section of newspapers usually indicate the current moon phase.

The sun is also significant. Preparing mixtures in the early morning, as close to dawn as possible, will bring gentle increases in power to the fragrance. A noon preparation time on the day of a full moon will lend you the power of combined solar and lunar energies. If you work at or after dusk, the darkness can absorb sorrow or pain. Any mixes you leave out on the eve of the summer solstice (set them out at dawn if you are an early riser) until noon the next day will be filled with the joy and optimism of this most magical day of all. (The date of the summer solstice varies from year to year but is around 21 June.)

Making flower waters

Flower waters are best made with fresh petals from a fragrant newly opened flower. The petals should be quite dry but not brown. Some recipes recommend bruising them first, while others (as I do) leave the petals intact. Bear in mind that the leaves of fragrant herbs are also suitable for making 'flower' waters, as are the flowers of the herbs chamomile (for riches, happiness, health and children) and lavender (for gentle love, peace and healing).

Lavender water is very good for helping children and adults facing bullying. Keep your flower waters on a shelf or in a cupboard in your indoor fragrant place.

The following recipe for rose water can be adapted to make a flower water from any scented petals or fresh herbs, though herbs tend to be best mixed with flowers. Rose and rosemary is my favourite combination. The quantities and timings are ones that work for me, but the art is to experiment as you make new batches, so you get the right quantities for the strength and fragrance you like. In fact, some of my best flower waters have been made when I was in a hurry and just threw everything in, shook well and then forgot the bottle for a few days. Keep notes of how you make your best batches.

Rose water recipe

Roses are one of the best flowers for making flower water and will bring love, self-esteem and healing into your world. The best roses for fragrance work are Rosa centifolia, most common as the big pink cabbage rose, and Rosa damescena, the dark red damask rose, but there are a number of other highly scented varieties. A visit to a garden centre or rose garden will give you the chance to identify the most fragrant.

This is one of a number of similar recipes and makes a rose water with a mild delicate fragrance, good for any occasion when you need self-love and self-confidence or seek to mend a quarrel. You can anoint yourself with the water, sprinkle it on your pillow or underwear, or carry it in a small bottle to smell just before an expected confrontation or when there has been a quarrel. You can also sprinkle a circle of rose water around yourself before going out if you feel under threat. Rose water can be used in your home for protection (see page 50), to represent Water on your altar (see pages 18–19) and for spiritual exploration, rituals and healing.

What you need: A medium-sized glass jar or wide-necked bottle with an airtight lid, a cup of distilled or mineral water (chilled), ¾ cup of rose petals, sprigs of rosemary or peppermint (optional), 2 or 3 drops of lavender or rose absolute essential oil or 1 drop of myrrh, 15 ml/1 tbsp 100% proof vodka, a funnel, a glass bottle with a stopper or screw-top lid, a pink rose-scented candle.

✧ Place the rose petals in the glass jar or wide-necked bottle and add the distilled or mineral water. Make sure the water covers the rose petals.

✧ Add the sprigs of rosemary or peppermint if you wish for a tangier fragrance (but if you do so, keep the same proportion of flowers to water).

✧ Add the lavender or rose absolute essential oil or the myrrh. This will enhance the fragrance.

✧ Stir in the vodka. Make sure there is only a small gap between the top of the liquid and the top of the jar and that the jar is securely watertight.

✧ Now put the lid on the jar and shake it, as you do so chanting the purpose of the water, for example:

> *I empower this water with self-esteem. May I be filled with self-love, self-confidence and inner radiance. So enter beauty into me, as I count to three. One, two, three. So may it be!* [Shake the mixture three more times] *Three, two, one* [shake again three times], *the mix is done.*

✧ Leave the mixture for at least 12 hours if possible. (You can use it earlier if the need is urgent.) To make the flower water stronger, leave it for two or three days, until the petals begin to brown. I shake my mixtures every few hours, repeating the chant, but some people prefer to leave well alone, so do whichever you prefer.

✧ When the time is up, use a small funnel to strain the mixture into the bottle with the stopper or screw-top lid. Seal the bottle and discard the petals.

✧ Before you use the rose water, light a pink rose-scented candle and repeat the empowerment. Allow the candle to burn down.

An alternative method for making flower waters

What you need: 2 cups of fresh flowers; a glass heatproof bowl; 1.2 litres/2 pints/2½ cups of water (preferably distilled); a non-metallic spoon; muslin, cheesecloth or a coffee filter, a wide-necked glass bottle with a lid or cork; 30 ml/2 tbsp 100% proof vodka.

✢ Put the flowers in the bowl. Boil the water and pour it on the flowers, stirring with the non-metallic spoon. As you do so, create an empowerment chant. For example, if you were using lavender, which is good after any kind of setback, loss or betrayal, you might say as you stirred:

Lavender of love, lavender of healing, heal my wounded heart and help me trust again.

✢ Cover the bowl and leave the flowers to infuse for 48 hours, stirring every six to eight hours and repeating the empowerment.

✢ When the time is up, strain the infusion into the wide-necked glass bottle through the muslin, cheesecloth or coffee filter. Discard the flowers.

✢ Stir the vodka into the bottle and shake it, repeating the empowerment, then cork or screw the lid on the bottle and store until it is needed.

To empower bought flower waters and colognes

✢ Shake the bottle of flower water or cologne gently nine times while reciting an appropriate chant of your own making.

✢ Add the bottle to your collection and empower it again before each use.

Infused oils

The original Ancient Egyptian perfumes were in the form of infused oils, containing no alcohol. Infused oils take longer to mature than flower waters – and the longer you steep them, the stronger the oil – but they are excellent for working towards any long-term goal. They can be added to your bath (a few drops) and used as massage oil (more dilute than essential oils, they do not need a carrier, but check on a small patch of skin that you are not allergic to the oil). The longer you steep petals or herbs in an infusion, the more fragrant the oil. Summer is a good time for making infused oils, because they need sunlight to mature.

The following recipe is for a rose oil, but you can use this method with any fragrant flower, for example lavender heads. You can also use fresh herb sprigs.

Making rose infused oil: an easy method

What you need: 2 large watertight and airtight jars or wide-necked bottles, sufficient extra-virgin olive oil and rose petals to almost fill one of them, muslin or cheesecloth, a dark glass bottle with a lid, a purple candle.

✣ Three-quarters fill the jar or wide-necked bottle with the olive oil and add the rose petals so they are entirely covered with the oil but not too tightly crammed. If necessary, add more oil and rose petals until the jar is almost full.

✣ Seal the jar and shake it, empowering the oil with suitable words of your own invention. For example:

> _Flower of beauty, thus infuse my life with joy; flower of light, so suffuse with loveliness my world that I may know delight._

✣ Set the jar in a sunny place or one where there is bright daylight for at least a few hours a day. Leave it for at least four weeks, shaking it each day and repeating the empowerment. (Rose infused oil will become pink when it is ready to be strained.)

✣ When the time is up, strain the petals through the muslin or cheesecloth into the second jar or wide-necked bottle, squeezing out every drop of oil you can.

✣ Pour the infused oil into the dark glass bottle, put on the lid and then repeat the empowerment, holding the bottle of oil between your hands.

✣ Keep the bottle in your indoor fragrant place until needed, at which time you can recite the empowerment for the final time, lighting the purple candle and letting it burn down. (You can empower the oil again every time you use it by shaking it nine times and reciting an appropriate chant of your own making.)

A method of making more intense infused oils

For an even more fragrant infused oil, prepare your oil as above until it is ready to be set in the sun.

✣ Empower your oil as described above.

✣ Do not shake the bottle, but whenever the petals become brown, remove them from the oil by straining them through muslin or cheesecloth (being careful to squeeze out as much oil as possible) and replacing them with fresh ones. You may need to do this a number of times, especially if there is a lack of sunlight. Empower the oil whenever you replace the petals.

✛ Repeat this process over six weeks, by the end of which a rose oil should be truly pink.

✛ Strain, bottle and empower your oil as described above.

Making a perfumed unguent

An unguent is more solid than an oil and can be rubbed in tiny amounts into the pulse points on your wrists or the psychic energy points in your palms and the soles of your feet to give you a feeling of confidence or peace of mind. Marigold (for protection against infidelity, help in legal matters, good luck and money), chamomile (for kindness, a gradual inflow of money, affection, friendship, family unity and protection), lavender (for happiness, peace, long life, love, protection and quiet sleep) and rose (for love, enchantment, psychic development, protection and healing from abuse) make especially good unguents.

What you need: 600 ml/1 pint/2½ cups infused perfumed oil, a ceramic or Pyrex saucepan, 15 ml/1 tbsp cocoa butter 50 g/2 oz beeswax, a wooden or ceramic spoon, a small glass pot with a lid or waxed paper.

✛ Heat the perfumed oil gently in the saucepan, but do not allow it to boil.

✛ Add the cocoa butter and beeswax and stir with the wooden or ceramic spoon until both have melted, repeating a short chant slowly and mesmerically, for example:

Marigold, marigold, bring me justice.

✛ Remove the pan from the heat and continue to stir until the mixture is thick and creamy and has cooled.

✛ Place the unguent in the pot, put on the lid or cover with the waxed paper and repeat the chant.

✛ Enchant the pot before use (see pages 31–2).

Making an essential oil water

What you need: 450 ml/³/₄ pt/2 cups of distilled water, a glass bowl, 30 ml/2 tbsp vodka, up to 20 drops of an essential oil of your choice, a glass or ceramic spoon, a small funnel, several small bottles with lids.

✢ Pour the distilled water into the glass bowl and add the vodka. Now add the essential oil, drop by drop, stopping when you have the strength of fragrance you require. With each drop you add, name a blessing or strength you seek, and stir the mixture between drops with the glass or ceramic spoon.

✢ Using the funnel, transfer the mixture to the small bottles. As you fill each one, name the fragrance and the purpose for which you made it, for example:

> _Juniper, juniper, fragrance of Fire, burn away what is destructive and painful and bring a new beginning for me._

A quick method of making an essential oil water

These sweet oils are good for anointing yourself.

What you need: 7–10 drops of your chosen essential oil, 30 ml/ 2 tbsp of a carrier oil such as sweet almond, olive or apricot, a small bottle with a lid.

✢ Pour the carrier oil into the small bottle and drop in the essential oil. Put on the lid and shake well.

Using fragrant oils for personal power

Fragrant oils can be used for personal empowerment without any additional ritual; however, when the energies of the four elements are also brought to bear, your oil will make you unstoppable!

An elemental ritual for courage

The basic method of this ritual comes from Ancient Egypt, where temple statues were daily anointed with different perfumes. I first used this particular ritual when I was making a necessary but risky career move at a time when the family was especially dependent on my income. You can adapt it for any purpose by choosing different fragrances (see pages 43–6 for a list of fragrances and their attributes).

What you need: A small bottle of each of the following flower waters or essential oil waters: geranium, lavender, orange/orange blossom (neroli)/frankincense, jasmine/rose; some fresh flowers of your choice; cotton wool balls; 4 small ceramic dishes; a dropper; a small empty bottle with a lid.

✢ Place the bottles of flower water or essential oil water in the appropriate quarter on the altar: geranium (for strength and fertility) in the North, lavender (for happiness and peace) in the East, orange or orange blossom (for self-confidence, good health, marriage partnerships, general well-being and abundance) or frankincense (for prosperity and success) in the South and jasmine (for intuition and harmony) or rose (for love and luck) in the West. Place the fresh flowers at the centre of the altar.

✢ Facing North, open the bottle of geranium and raise it, turning to all four directions in turn and stating the power you seek from the fragrance. For example:

Geranium, give me the power to be strong and make my ideas fertile to attract success.

✢ Inhale the scent and place a single drop on your brow. Then place a drop on a cotton wool ball and put it in a dish in the North, saying:

With geranium I purify this altar and my work. May only goodness and light enter within.

✢ Facing East, open the bottle of lavender and raise it, turning to all four directions and stating the power you need from the fragrance. For example:

Lavender, heal my fears of past failure and grant my wish for new outlets across the seas.

✢ Inhale the scent and place a single drop at the centre of your throat. Then place a drop on a cotton wool ball and put it in a dish in the East, saying:

With lavender I purify this altar and my work. May only goodness and light enter within.

✢ Facing South, open the bottle of orange, orange blossom or frankincense water and raise it, turning to all four directions and stating the power you need from the fragrance. For example:

Orange, bring me abundance of resources and the confidence to strive for what I really want.

✢ Inhale the scent and place a single drop on your left wrist. Then place a drop on a cotton wool ball and put it in a dish in the South, saying:

With orange (orange blossom/frankincense) I purify this altar and my work. May only goodness and light enter within.

✢ Facing West, open the bottle of jasmine or rose water and raise it, turning to all four directions and stating the power you need from the fragrance. For example:

Jasmine, bring me intuitive awareness of the right times to act and when to wait and be silent.

✢ Inhale the scent and place a single drop on your right wrist. Then place a drop on a cotton wool ball and put it in a dish in the West, saying:

With jasmine (rose) I purify this altar and my work. May only goodness and light enter within.

✢ Finally, using the dropper, take fragrance from each of the four bottles in turn and add it to the empty bottle. Put on the lid, shake it and place it in the centre of the altar next to the flowers, saying:

So mingle, you Earth, Air, Water, Fire, to join in me a greater power to bring what I desire.

✢ Leave the bottle on the altar until the event for which it was created. Then apply it, repeating the final chant.

Fragrances and personality types

There are countless ways of characterising fragrances – the following is just one method. I have found it useful for categorising aromas that resonate naturally with certain people.

Floral

✢ Those with an affinity for floral fragrances are naturally

No

optimistic, eternally romantic, gentle and loving. They are appreciative of beautiful things but incredibly generous, sometimes too much for their own good.

✢ Other types can use florals to open themselves to love and to counter workaholic tendencies.

✢ Floral fragrances include chamomile, hyacinth, jasmine, lavender, linden blossom, marigold, mimosa, orange blossom (neroli) – sometimes categorised as citrus–sweet, rose and ylang ylang.

Citrus

✢ Those with an affinity for citrus fragrances are open-minded, ready to change, intelligent, witty and sometimes sharp-tongued. They are eager for travel and new experiences.

✢ Other types can use citrus for the courage to try new things and to sharpen their communicative and learning skills.

✢ Citrus fragrances include bergamot, grapefruit, lemon, lemongrass, lime, orange, and tangerine.

Herbaceous

✢ Those with an affinity for herbaceous fragrances are compassionate, caring and concerned for the environment. They are also vulnerable, patient with others and accept that everything has its time and season.

✢ Other types can use herbaceous scents to add idealism and integrity to money-making plans and to get more in touch with the natural world.

✢ Herbaceous fragrances include basil, clary sage, fennel, hyssop, marjoram, rosemary, sage and thyme.

Leaves

✢ Those with an affinity for leaf fragrances are natural healers and express their creativity in doing rather than speaking. They are wise and experienced in the ways of the world and make any place homelike and welcoming.

✢ Other types can use leafy fragrances to help them to settle down and to ground ideas in practical expression.

✧ Leaf fragrances include bay, cypress, eucalyptus, myrtle, patchouli, pine and tea tree

Roots

✧ Those with an affinity for root fragrances are rooted in reality and in the rich traditions of the past. They are slow to speak in anger or to act impulsively, trustworthy, loyal and amazingly good with money.

✧ Other types can use root fragrances before entering into contracts, any form of speculation, or matters concerning material security or property.

✧ Root fragrances include angelica, ginger – sometimes categorised as a spice – turmeric, valerian and vetivert.

Spices

✧ Those with an affinity for spice fragrances are quicksilver, full of passion and fire, inspired by ideas, eager to explore what lies beyond the horizon, courageous, individualistic and inventive. They are always able to turn a reversal into an advantage and maximise any opportunity.

✧ Other types can use spice fragrances for courage, impetus for change, good luck in financial speculation, to initiate action and to cut through inertia.

✧ Spice fragrances include allspice, anise, cinnamon, cloves, coriander (cilantro), frankincense, myrrh, nutmeg and peppermint.

Sweet

✧ Those with an affinity for sweet fragrances are sensual, relaxed, charismatic, sociable, faithful, fertile in ideas, open-hearted, sympathetic and harmonious. They are natural communicators, eager to see the best and to create happiness and well-being, and are able to bring different kinds of people together.

✧ Other types can use sweet fragrances for positive energy when undertaking negotiations or attempting to reconcile different demands on their time and when it is necessary to exercise tolerance with difficult people.

✣ Sweet fragrances include apricot, geran~~i~~
melissa (lemon balm), violet and vanilla.

Woody

✣ Those with an affinity for woody fragrances a~~re~~
and leaders. They are idealistic, seeing the glo~~bal~~
than the personal view, able to take a long-term ~~p~~
guide others, and good at starting over again an~~d~~
the past.

✣ Other types can use woody fragrances for positive ~~energ~~y when
starting over again, after reversals and when a goal seems a long
way off and it is necessary to persevere.

✣ Woody fragrances include cedarwood, rosewood, juniper and
sandalwood.

Creating your own personality mix

You can use the categories above to create your own personal
fragrance. If, for example, you are a floral type, experiment with
blending floral oils until you find a combination that is right for
you. As you read through the fragrance types above, you may have
discovered that you fit into more than one category. In this case,
blend oils from each relevant category in the proportion that is
right for your personality. Once you have your special blend, use it
for a sudden burst of optimism or to strengthen your confidence
when you are under attack, being criticised or just feeling wobbly.
It can also stand in on occasions when your signature fragrance
might be too formal.

You can also add drops of specific oils to your basic personality
blend that will temporarily boost your personality with the
particular qualities you need at particular times. Thus dreamy
floral people may occasionally need a touch of spice to make them
more assertive and able to reach for what they want rather than
always letting others ahead in the queue of life. On the other hand,
a sharp-witted and acid-tongued citrus type may need an
occasional herbaceous touch of gentleness in dealing with
vulnerable people.

Your personality mix

You can use the instructions for the essential oil water on page 41 to make your personality mix. Alternatively, you can follow this quick method.

What you need: A selection of essential oils from the category/ies above that you fall into, a medium-sized bottle of carrier oil, a dropper, some bowls or saucers, a small bottle with a lid.

✢ Experiment with combinations of the oils you have chosen by dropping tiny amounts into a teaspoonful of carrier oil in a bowl or saucer. Make as many different blends as you need to until you are satisfied that you have made a fragrance that reflects your personality.

✢ When you have your blend, keeping the original proportions, make up a bottle of fragrance, using 7–10 drops of essential oil to 30 ml/2 tbsp of carrier oil.

✢ Bottle your fragrance, shake it well and empower it, following the instructions on pages 27–31.

Making oils to modify your personality mix

If you have a blend of oils to hand from each of the eight categories listed on pages 43–6, you can modify your own personality mix at any time by adding a few drops of another personality blend to give you qualities that you need. For example, if you need a boost to your financial acumen, you might try adding a spicy peppermint combination to your own sweet geranium-based personality mix.

Apply only a single drop of the new personality mix in anointing. Be careful with the spices and citruses as these can be astringent. Do not apply them to delicate parts of the body. If you prefer, you can just inhale the new fragrance or put a few drops on a small piece of silk to carry with you in a purse.

What you need: A selection of essential oils or essential oil waters from each of the categories on pages 43–6, a dropper, eight small bottles with lids, a large bottle of carrier oil, some bowls or saucers (optional).

✢ Experiment with combinations of the oils you have chosen within each category by dropping tiny amounts into a teaspoonful of carrier oil in a saucer. When you are satisfied with the fragrance, keeping the original proportions, make up a bottle of the blend, using 7–10 drops of essential oil to 30 ml/2 tbsp of carrier oil.

✢ Bottle each of your blends, shake them well and keep them safely for use on occasions when you need to modify your personality mix for a particular purpose.

Using a pendulum to modify your personality mix

This is a great method if you are uncertain of the right mix for the particular quality you need.

What you need: Oils made for modifying your personality mix (see instructions above), a crystal pendulum, some of your personality mix in a small bottle with a lid.

✢ Set the oils in a circle.

✢ Hold the pendulum over each bottle in turn, asking to be shown which is the right fragrance to add to your basic personality mix for your current need. The pendulum will feel heavy and pull downwards over the one that will be helpful right now.

✢ Add the oils indicated by the pendulum to the bottle of personality mix. Put the lid on and shake it well. Empower your new fragrance by naming the purpose for which it is intended.

CHAPTER 4

Fragrance in the Home and Workplace

For thousands of years herbal fragrances have been used to create a psychic barrier against negative or harmful forces entering dwelling places. The Native North Americans, for instance, used the fragrant smoke of sagebrush, sweetgrass and cedar smudge sticks to protect their homes, their possessions and themselves. Many of these psychically protective herbs were also used for their practical protective properties. For example, basil and eau de cologne mint were hung from ceilings to repel flies, while lavender and rosemary were used to banish fleas. Eau de cologne mint was also traditionally put on babies' cots to keep insects away.

Down the centuries, aromatic herbs and flowers have also been kept in the house or grown in the garden to attract happiness, health, prosperity and good fortune. In the modern home these, together with more exotic fragrances, may still be found in the form of oils and incenses, scented candles and hot-house flowers. In workplaces, too, essential oils are increasingly being used to reduce tensions and increase harmony and efficiency.

Fragrant protection of the home

Many of the traditional protective remedies from the folk magic of western and eastern Europe and Scandinavia travelled with early settlers to America, Canada, Australia, New Zealand and South Africa, sometimes mingling with indigenous customs. In particular, settlers from Ireland carried with them to America herbs and even parts of trees such as the sacred ash, which gave protection against snakes. The following folklore is common to a number of lands.

✤ Entry points to a home were traditionally considered vulnerable to penetration by negative influences, and aromatic bay trees were frequently planted near entrances to filter out all harm and to ensure that prosperity, good fortune and domestic happiness were attracted to the dwelling. For modern flat-dwellers, small pot varieties of bay tree are available, and these are still a very powerful filter of the day's stress. If they are outside, the rain will wash them clean. If they are kept indoors, try to take them out occasionally when it rains. In hotter climates lemon trees served the same purpose as bay.

✝ Dill was often hung over doorways and above infants' cradles or scattered around the boundaries of a home to protect against malice and envy.

✝ Lilac bushes and honeysuckle were grown up external walls to keep domestic happiness within and repel all whose envy would spoil it (see page 57).

✝ The herb catnip was grown near front doors to attract good fortune and benign forces and repel thieves. (It also makes cats, even old ones, incredibly frisky.)

✝ Chopped and dried nettles, surprisingly aromatic, were scattered across thresholds to absorb negativity and deter intruders – earthly and paranormal – and sharp-tongued or jealous visitors. I buy dried nettles from a local grocer and keep a small pot of them at the side of the doorstep, sheltered from the rain. I replace them regularly, scattering the old ones to the winds, well away from the house so that the negativity they have absorbed will not blow back in.

✝ Door knobs and external window sills were traditionally anointed on the first day of spring with a few drops of home-made rose or lavender water (see pages 36–8) while a chant was recited, for example: 'May nothing dark enter here, harm or hostility, only peace, tranquillity and blessings to this my sanctuary.' This annual anointing ritual is equally effective against modern ills and intruders. In view of increased pollution, noise and stress in daily life, you may decide also to anoint inside window sills and doorknobs, afterwards opening all the doors and windows to let in the spring. You can, of course, use commercially prepared rose or lavender water.

Protection indoors

Protection indoors forms a second line of defence against external threats and negativity that may enter with visitors or stressed-out family members coming home from school or work. It is also useful for absorbing bad atmospheres from worries or quarrels, which may hang around even when these have been resolved, provoking further irritation and testiness. Here are a few indoor protection ideas.

✢ In the kitchen hang cloves of garlic still on the string. These will absorb bad feelings, quarrels, sadness and anxiety as well as any negativity left over from the day. (Do not use the defensive garlic for cooking, but bury it every few weeks and replace it with fresh cloves.) Alternatively, you can hang bunches of the flowering wild garlic (which has a more subtle scent) from the kitchen ceiling.

✢ Lavender, bay, pine, sage and rosemary were traditionally burned on an open grate in the main hearth to remove negative feelings, repel sickness and attract health and harmony to the family home. If you do not have an open fire, burn a mixture of these fragrances as essential oil in a burner or as scented candles to make use of their protective and positive qualities.

Protective sprays

An instant way of clearing bad vibes and creating ongoing protection (perhaps prior to a challenging family gathering or to ensure a period of relaxation when the family come home after a stressful day) is to use an essential-oil-based spray. Essential oil sprays are more environmentally friendly than chemical-laden aerosol sprays and also neutralise rather than mask pet smells and other unwanted aromas.

To make an essential oil spray, simply fill a pump action spray bottle (of the kind used for watering plants) with half a litre (1 scant pint) of water and add 10–15 drops of essential oil. Shake the mixture before releasing it into the atmosphere, naming the purpose for which it was created (for example, tranquillity, peace or protection).

✢ Spray a harmonising fragrance such as chamomile, jasmine, melissa (lemon balm), orange blossom (neroli), rose, lavender or ylang ylang if difficult relatives are calling or there are ongoing family personality clashes.

✢ If you need a more potent neutraliser of negativity, try bergamot, eucalyptus, lemongrass, peppermint, pine or thyme. These oils will also encourage optimism and positive communication between family members.

✢ Citronella is excellent not only for keeping away flying insects (try it in scented candles and torches for the garden) but also for deterring over-curious neighbours, visitors who outstay their welcome and emotional 'vampires'.

✢ Rosewood is good for easing tense atmospheres and relaxing stressed individuals, especially if volatile teenagers or adults with mid-life crises are present in the home. It helps to soften potential criticism or sarcasm and to counter unwanted mood swings, hormonal or otherwise.

✢ If sadness, resentment or lethargy has penetrated the house, make a stimulating essential oil mixture containing three drops of orange, two drops of lemon, three drops of lemongrass and three drops of lime or melissa (lemon balm) in half a litre (1 scant pint) of water. Spray as a fine mist in living areas.

Pot pourri as a harmoniser
One of the best ways of maintaining an atmosphere of long-lasting peace and well-being in your home is by using bowls of appropriately scented pot pourri.

Pot pourri is slow-acting and gradually builds up its energies, keeping its fragrance for several weeks. This fragrance can be restored by adding essential or fragranced oils to the dried flowers and herbs. However, some people, myself included, believe that when the natural scent of pot pourri fades, the harmonising and protective function of the pot pourri has likewise diminished and the mix should be replaced.

You can buy pot pourri ready mixed in department stores, houseware stores and supermarkets. Most varieties have a dominant ingredient that will indicate the main characteristic of the mix, so you can choose the kind that your home currently needs, for example rose for healing and harmony, lavender for gentle energies, pine for removing negativity, sandalwood for protection and healing, peach for fertility and abundance, vanilla for a sense of contentment and balance, and so on.

You can sometimes find elemental pot pourri mixes on sale, in Earth, Air, Fire and Water packs. (A large UK/US supermarket chain sells these.) They can restore the balance to a home or particular room. For example, if there are a lot of temper tantrums or confrontations, or if there are a lot of minor accidents in the home, you may be suffering from an excess of the Fire element and need a counterbalancing Water pot pourri, containing ingredients such as peach, hyacinth, jasmine, lemon, vanilla and violet. If, on the other hand, everyone in the home is feeling exhausted or weighed down by too much responsibility or money worries, or there has been a lot of minor illness, an uplifting Air pot pourri will lighten the mood. This might include ingredients such as almond, bergamot, lavender, lemon verbena, marjoram and peppermint. If everyone is snappy and can't relax or sleep, there may be an excess of Air and you will benefit from an Earth mix, including such ingredients as fern, geranium, heather, hibiscus, honeysuckle and mimosa. And if feelings or hormones are churning and every decision or request is turned into a three-act drama, you have an excess of Water in the home and need some counterbalancing Fire pot pourri, containing such ingredients as basil, carnation, marigold, orange blossom and rosemary.

Drying herbs and flowers for pot pourri

The following method is very quick and easy. You can find other methods in books (see Useful Reading).

Flowers suitable for pot pourri include carnations, chamomile, cornflowers, freesias, jasmine, heliotrope, honeysuckle, lavender, lilac, lilies, lily of the valley, pinks, poppies, stocks of all colours and roses. Herbs include basil, lavender, lemon verbena, marjoram, melissa (lemon balm), mint, rosemary, sage and thyme.

Fixatives (to preserve the fragrance of your dried flowers and herbs) include powdered frankincense, myrrh and orris root; salt; and sandalwood, clary sage and oregano essential oil (use just a few drops).

What you need: Herbs and flowers of your choice; a piece of muslin, cheesecloth or a similar porous material stretched over a frame; enough wide jars with lids to store your herbs and flowers (airproof kitchen storage containers are ideal); some salt; some orris root; sticky labels.

✤ If possible, remove the leaves and flowers from the stems of your chosen plants. If they are too delicate, they can be removed when dry.

✤ Spread the leaves and flowers in a single layer on the frame. Keep them in separate areas of the frame (or have a series of small frames) because different species will take different times to dry – anything from a few days to two or three weeks roughly. If you live in a hot dry climate, the time will be much shorter. They are dry when they have a papery texture but retain their colour and fragrance. Place the frame in a warm, dry area away from sunlight – do not use artificial heat. If you are drying lavender or herbs with strong stems, you can hang them from the ceiling or on hooks, in a room with a north-facing light.

✤ When a species of herb or flower is dry, place a layer of it in one of the storage jars. Sprinkle it with about half a teaspoon each of salt and orris root. Then add another layer, again sprinkling it with salt and orris root. Carry on layering in this way until the jar is full. Then screw the lid on tightly and label it with the date and contents.

✤ Store the herbs or flowers in the dark for about three weeks, after which they will be ready to use.

Making pot pourri

You can make your own elemental pot pourri recipes using the lists on pages 17–9 as a guide. Alternatively, you may prefer to create pot pourri for more general purposes such as calming or energising different rooms. For example, you could have a carnation/lilac/orange/lemon/rosemary mix in the dining room to stimulate lively but loving conversation, or a rose-based mix in the bedroom for peaceful dreams.

Some department stores and craft shops sell dried flowers in separate tubs so you can choose your own ready-dried pot pourri ingredients. If you want to keep dried petals you have bought this way, you can add a fixative (see page 53) and store them in airtight jars. If a fixative has already been included (check the contents), you don't need to add anything before storing. If you would like to dry your own herbs and flowers, follow the instructions above. You can also add such ingredients as dried pine needles, vanilla pods and cedar wood or sandalwood chips, and ground spices including allspice, cinnamon, cloves, juniper berries, ginger, mace and nutmeg.

If your pot pourri is intended to enhance the atmosphere of your home, encourage family members to join in the mixing. When you have made your pot pourri, make a note in your journal of mixes and proportions that work well.

What you need: Some fresh orange, lime or lemon peel; dried herbs and flowers and ground spices of your choice; a small glass or ceramic bowl; a large glass or ceramic bowl; a wooden or ceramic spoon; 6–8 drops of a fragrant essential oil such as lavender, lemon, orange, geranium, orange blossom (neroli) or rose; 15 ml/1 tbsp of a fixing powder or 6 drops of a fixing oil (see page 53); enough dark airtight jars to contain your finished pot pourri (each jar will be only half-filled).

✤ A few hours before making the pot pourri, dry the orange, lime or lemon peel in a low oven for about 10 minutes (or a microwave for about a minute). This will add extra vitality to the mix. (Citrus is especially good in pot pourri for sickrooms and rooms used by pets.)

✤ First of all experiment with the fragrance by combining a few petals or leaves of different species at a time in the small bowl, removing any that overpower or clash with others. Take time to get the mix right for you.

✤ When you have your basic mix, put the ingredients into the large bowl in proportions of roughly three cups of dried flowers and leaves to 50 grams/two tablespoonfuls of powdered spice. Increase or decrease the relative quantities to your taste. If you want a predominant flower or fragrance add that in a three to two proportion to all the other ingredients.

✤ When you are satisfied with the fragrance, mix well with a wooden spoon, reciting as a chant the purpose for which the pot pourri is being made – whether for general protection and harmony, or for someone who is sick, or for a room that feels dark and negative.

÷ Add the drops of essential oil for extra fragrance and mix again, repeating the chant or adding blessings and perhaps naming family members and their individual needs. Any family members or friends who are helping can make wishes for one another.

÷ Finally, add the fixing powder or fixing oil and mix again. If you like, you can recite this very old folk chant:

One for joy and two for gladness, three and four away with sadness, five and six to banish pain, seven, eight, nine bring peace/joy again.

÷ Fill the jars half-full with pot pourri (so that you can shake them regularly and let the pot pourri mix). Put the lids on tightly and leave the pot pourri in a darkened place for several weeks. Shake it regularly – if you are in a hurry, frequent shaking will cut down the necessary storage time. The pot pourri is ready when it is fragrant but not sticky.

A fragrant garden for protection and empowerment

At the beginning of this chapter I talked about how plants placed outside an external door can provide positive energy and psychic protection. In fact the whole garden, back as well as front, creates a protective filter against negativity from the world while at the same time acting as a repository for good fortune, health and prosperity to the home and all who live there. Five or 10 minutes in the garden in the early morning before work or in the evening, even in the dark, restores natural harmony to your mind and body and fills you with the different strengths of the flowers and herbs growing there, especially if you breathe slowly and deeply. The early mediaeval mystic Hildegard von Bingen (who invented lavender water) called this 'the greening principle'.

If you do not have a garden, you can set protective fragrant plants on window ledges and indoors against the four external walls (counting party walls as external). You can also use balconies and shared lobbies to set up your barriers against external negativity. I

otective garden consisting entirely of plants
r-city terraced yard.

ɔlace (see pages 19–20) can form the centre
ι empowering garden. You can also design
:as (of even a small garden) with herbs that
; that will enrich your life and that of your
-size of the plot and the quantity of herbs do
y pot of basil will drive away irrational fears
ak if you are alone in the house late at night!

recently been restored after an assault by
ɟ every available inch of it with cement and
g catastrophe has enabled me to create a
planned magical aromatic garden with a tree in the centre, on
which I hang waterproof bags of dried herbs for different purposes
(such as healing), ribbons with thanks for blessings received and
requests for myself and other people, and various small fertility
baskets. I always try to give visitors a sachet, ribbon or other gift
from the tree.

The following is a summary of the plants I have in my garden,
some of which you might like to plant. My garden is quite small
and is long and narrow (my home was once described by a snooty
newspaper reporter as Coronation-Street-on-Sea) but I have been
able to fit in all the herbs with the qualities my home needs.

✢ **Angelica** drives off fears and phantoms of the night and attracts
good luck in work for family members. Angelica is often set at the
four corners of a house to turn back intruders and guard against
storm damage.

✢ **Basil** is another anti-fear plant. It also draws in money,
especially if coins are buried at its base.

✢ **Chamomile** protects children from hurt and brings sunshine
into the home, countering teenage moodiness and adult angst.

✢ **Fennel** deters unwanted door-to-door salespeople and critical
visitors, and gives the courage to fight for those who are dear.

✢ **Honeysuckle** is the doorkeeper, turning away doubts and fears
and keeping vulnerable family members safe within. It is good
against teenagers' friends who may wield an undesirable influence.

✧ **Jasmine** counters the stresses of the modern world, offering a gentle reconnection with the natural cycles of life and seasonal ebbs and flows.

✧ **Lavender** stops troublesome neighbours in their tracks, preventing gossip and turning carping into kindness.

✧ **Mimosa** absorbs sadness and brings a sense of harmony and well-being to the home and garden.

✧ **Orange and lemon trees** balance defensive and welcoming energies so that those with good intentions will feel happy in your home but any who come with spite will be unable to settle and will leave quickly.

✧ **Parsley** guards against misfortune and the draining away of resources. It is good against floods – of both the bathroom and the natural variety.

✧ **Roses** bring love, while their thorns act as a physical and psychic barrier against harm.

✧ **Rosemary** is a guardian against thieves and vandals and assures that there will be sufficient resources for the home and family.

✧ **Sage** cleanses dark thoughts and brings optimism on the blackest of days

✧ **Thyme** takes away regrets about what cannot be resolved and brings enthusiasm for every new day.

✧ **Wild garlic** repels harmful spirits and also brings healing, especially when the white flowers are in full bloom in May.

Many of the herbs I suggest above can be found worldwide, sometimes under different folk names. If you need to identify them, you will find the Latin names in the list on pages 171–80. You may also find that the area where you live has its own protective herbs. Check local folklore books or ask at an established garden centre where they grow their own plants.

Workplace protection

In agricultural societies where workshops were attached to houses or people worked in the fields, herbs and flowers were readily available and pollution was very low. In a modern urban or technological setting we are often divorced from the natural protection of fragrant plants, especially if we work in a city or an industrial unit. Air conditioning, the constant jangle of phones and faxes, neon lighting and the competitive – even hostile – atmosphere that often occurs in a workplace can lead to headaches, muscle tension, stress and fatigue.

There are a number of ways you can counter these ills and bring fragrant protection and empowerment to your workplace.

✢ On your desk, workbench or another suitable area, set two or three small dishes of dried herbs, for example sage, dried chamomile flowers, thyme or fennel seeds. Place them near the front of the workspace, where tension and intrusions enter, or near your phone/fax. Replace the herbs every three or four days, or more frequently if there has been a tense period or a lot of gossip. Cast the old herbs to the winds in any open space.

✢ If you have room, exchange the traditional odourless green office plants for miniature orange trees, which will increase self-esteem and so lower aggressive competition.

✢ Also consider tiny bays for protection and loyalty between workers, pots of lavender and miniature roses for healing old quarrels and rivalries, and a pot of sage to counter sick office syndrome, in which large numbers of staff are frequently absent with stress or minor ailments.

✢ Essential oils can also restore the balance in the workplace. Add a couple of drops of oil to a cup of warm water and place it on your desk or workbench. Replace the oil regularly. If you sit near a radiator, you can balance a saucer of oil in water on top of it or drop some oil onto a cotton wool ball and put it on the radiator. Try protective pine if you need to send back negative vibes and encourage happy interactions. Eucalyptus repels spite and improves general office health. Tea tree will cleanse the environment of malice and increase productivity (good if you are self-employed or paid by results). Orange, orange blossom (neroli) and lemon verbena are excellent for creating an atmosphere of optimism and for silencing moaners.

Smoking out the bad vibes

If your workplace is unfriendly or you have a haranguing boss, try smoke cleansing. This is one of the most effective ways of dispelling a negative atmosphere and creating more helpful interactions. You can use a traditional Native American smudge stick, usually consisting of dried sagebrush and available in New Age stores and healthfood shops, or a sage incense stick.

Of course, you might cause a certain amount of alarm if you began walking round your workplace with a lighted smudge stick chanting. What is more, you would be likely to set off the smoke arms and arouse the scepticism of those who are usually the ones giving off the most negative vibes. However, psychic powers do not need direct physical correspondences, so the cleansing will be just as effective if you draw a map of your office and smudge it at home. Make your map large and use flame-retardant paper. You can use separate sheets to indicate the various floors or departments. Include lifts, doors, windows, partitions and the desks or workbenches of yourself and your colleagues, labelling them and emphasising with dark colours the space of anyone who is particularly spiteful or who drains enthusiasm. Alternatively, you could draw your map in the sand in a child's sand box, in the earth with a stick, or with chalk on an uncarpeted floor or outside in a yard.

What you need: A sagebrush smudge stick or sage incense stick, a map of your workplace, some dried culinary sage.

✦ Light the smudge stick or incense, as you do so saying:

May peace alone remain and harmony; though many meet,
let enmity be none. Quarrels and fear be gone!

Smudge sticks should be lit at one end and then carefully blown out so that the end glows red. If necessary, blow gently on the tip to get the smoke flowing in a steady stream. You can relight the stick if it goes out. Use your power hand (the one you write with) to hold the smudge stick and fan the smoke with the other hand, first of all making anticlockwise spirals to remove negativity and then making a counterbalancing clockwise smudge to infuse positive energies.

✢ Begin at the main entrance on your chart and then continue from the top of the building downwards, floor by floor, concentrating on areas where negative energies can filter through, including the lift door and the staircase. Then smudge again, working from the main entrance round in a circle and moving inwards. As you smudge say:

All calm, naught harm. Be at peace, hostility cease. Harmony enter those who are troubled or trouble the well-being of the office/store/factory.

Focus your attention on any problematic desks or work stations, making double smoke spirals in both directions over any workspace occupied by a difficult colleague and a triple spiral in both directions over the workspace of any senior colleague or employer who is being bullying or autocratic. Remember to smudge a clockwise circle of protection around your own work area.

✢ Finally, draw a clockwise circle round the whole area you have smudged, saying:

Keep light always within, and loveliness, laughter and life.

✢ Place the plan where it will remain clean and uncreased. Surround it with a circle of the dried culinary sage. You can re-smudge whenever tensions or problems arise.

You can also smudge your home, walking round each room in turn. (See page 182 for details of books on smudging.)

CHAPTER 5

Personal Energy Work with Fragrance

In this chapter we will work with ways of using fragrance to create a sense of well-being and maximise your potential both spiritually and mentally. Fragrances can also be used for cleansing the personal negativity that we accumulate from daily life and work, for filtering out hostility and spite, and for restoring harmony to our mind, body and spirit.

Fragrance and the chakra system

The chakra system, which has common roots in India and Africa, suggests that there are spiritual energy centres, known in the Indian system as chakras, throughout the body. These act as channels through which we receive the life force from the cosmos, from the earth and from plants, flowers and trees. Whether or not you accept the concept of chakras as literally true, it can be a useful way to picture and understand your energy system symbolically as you work with it. If you want to know more about the chakras, there are a number of books on this way of conceptualising and healing our personal energy system, including my own *Chakra Power* (see page 181 for details).

It is hypothesised that we possess seven main chakras or energy centres (see diagram on page 64). As well as receiving the life force and natural energies from the external world, these chakras absorb impressions, thoughts and feelings from other people and from the environment in which we live. These energy receivers can therefore become clogged up with daily stress and pollution from the modern technological and industrial world as well as from any negative encounters we have with other people. You will know that your chakras are blocked if you feel out of sorts, tired, sluggish and lethargic. Chakras are, of course, energised by positive interactions, a good work and home life and the occasional day in the countryside or garden.

Chakras can also be over-stimulated by hyped-up people, noisy workplaces and crowded trains or motorways, as well as too much caffeine, fast food, tobacco, alcohol or additived. (There are, of course, chemicals in commercial perfumes and you may choose to use only natural fragrances; however, in my opinion the chemical additives contained in manufactured perfumes are in such small quantities that they cannot be compared with major pollutants.) You will know that your chakras are in overdrive if you feel irritable and unable to relax even if you are tired. Fortunately, fragrances are very effective cleansers and restorers of stressed or malfunctioning chakras. Aromatic herbs, oils and incenses are powerful transmitters of positive healing energies from the earth to our body, mind and inner spiritual core. Applying fragrances to particularly sensitive points on the body can trigger a powerful positive response. Try it and see for yourself. In my own experience, it can balance the most stressed and exhausted body and still a racing mind.

While I was researching in Cairo, I discovered that each of the seven main chakras has its own individual associated fragrance that is effective for cleansing, balancing and empowering. These associations are based on a very old African system that was developed to a high level of sophistication in Ancient Egypt. Much of this knowledge is now transmitted only orally in Egypt, out of respect for the prevailing religious culture.

In the following description, the chakras are described in ascending order, but you can also approach them from the top down. Remember that these are psychic rather than physical power centres, and they can vary subtly in position from person to person. If you hold the palm of your power hand over each of the areas shown in the diagram on page 64, you may feel a swirling. This indicates the centre of your own chakra.

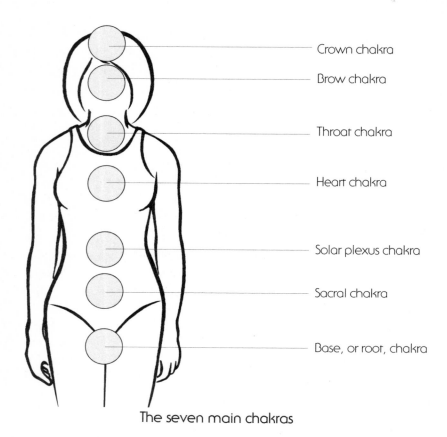

Crown chakra

Brow chakra

Throat chakra

Heart chakra

Solar plexus chakra

Sacral chakra

Base, or root, chakra

The seven main chakras

The base, or root, chakra

✦ This is the chakra of the earth. It is located at the base of the spine and absorbs earth energy through the perineum when we sit on the ground. It also operates via two smaller psychic energy points in the soles of the feet.

✦ It rules the legs, feet, large intestine and skeleton, including the teeth.

✦ Imbalances can be reflected as pain and tension in any of the body parts this chakra rules, as constipation or irritable bowel symptoms, as a general lack of energy, a tendency to minor accidents, or an inability to relax even when exhausted.

✦ On a psychological level unreasonable anger or paralysing fear from trivial causes can be a symptom of a blockage.

✢ Visualise circular beams of rich red light emanating from this chakra. Also visualise these beams rising from the earth and into your body.

Base/root chakra fragrances
✢ The main fragrance is mimosa. Others include cedar, cedarwood, cinnamon, hyacinth, patchouli, rosewood and vetivert. (Cinnamon can be an irritant, so use only 2 drops of essential oil per 30 ml/2 tbsp of carrier oil and test on a small patch of skin beforehand.)

✢ Using a single drop of fragrance, anoint either the soles of your feet, your ankle bones or the small of your back. Do not anoint the perineum itself, as it is too delicate.

Sacral chakra
✢ This is the chakra of the moon. It is seated in the sacrum/lower abdomen, around the reproductive system.

✢ It rules the blood, all bodily fluids, hormones, the reproductive system, the kidneys, the circulation and the bladder.

✢ Blockages can manifest as fluid retention, menstrual or menopausal problems, mood swings, impotence in men and an inability to relax in sex for women.

✢ Psychological problems involve seeking emotional satisfaction through physical indulgence (especially in food) and other oral-related issues.

✢ Visualise spheres of golden orange light emanating from this chakra. Also visualise light flowing inwards as silver moonbeams, even if the moon is not shining.

Sacral chakra fragrances
✢ The main fragrance is jasmine. Other sacral fragrances include apricot, coconut, eucalyptus, hibiscus, lemon, lilac, melissa (lemon balm), myrrh, musk (use synthetic) and ylang ylang. (Avoid even diluted myrrh oil for anointing, as it can be an irritant to sensitive parts.)

✢ Using a single drop of fragrance, anoint above the genitals or around the womb, on the lower abdomen.

Solar plexus chakra

✢ This is the chakra of fire, and it is situated above the navel, around the central stomach area.

✢ It controls digestion, the liver, the spleen, the gall bladder, the stomach, the small intestine and the metabolism.

✢ Blockages and malfunctions can manifest as digestive disorders, hyperactivity or a sluggish metabolism. Lowered resistance to minor illnesses and slower recovery can also result from imbalances in this chakra.

✢ On a psychological level, lack of self-confidence, obsessions, inability to concentrate, constant fault-finding and failure to empathise with others can result from the inefficient working of this chakra.

✢ Visualise clear yellow rays of light like morning sunshine radiating from this area. Also see these rays radiating from the sun and onto your body, even on cloudy days.

Solar plexus fragrances

✢ The main solar plexus fragrance is frankincense. Others include chamomile, carnation, honeysuckle, lemon verbena, marigold, orange blossom (neroli) and peppermint. (Frankincense can be an irritant, so dilute it extra well, 3–5 drops per 30 ml/2 tbsp carrier oil, or substitute another fragrance such as chamomile if your skin is sensitive.)

✢ Using a single drop of fragrance, anoint the centre of your stomach, midway between navel and chest.

Heart chakra

✢ This is the chakra of the winds and is in the centre of the chest.

✢ It rules the heart, lungs and breasts, and also the hands and arms, as well as the minor chakras in the centre of the palms of the hands, which are used in enchantment (see pages 31–2).

✢ Constant coughs, breathing difficulties and allergies result from a blockage or imbalance in this chakra.

✢ Mood swings, over-sensitivity to the problems of others, panic attacks, anxiety and depression can result from malfunctions.

✦ Picture rich bright green light flowing out of your hands, heart and chest. Also visualise green light flowing into your body from plants, flowers and trees.

Heart chakra fragrances
✦ The main heart fragrance is rose. Others include apple blossom, geranium, hyacinth, lilac, lily of the valley, peach, strawberry and vervain.

✦ Using a single drop of fragrance, anoint the centre of your chest or the palms of your hands (one drop on each).

Throat chakra
✦ This is the chakra of sound. It is situated in the centre of the neck, close to the Adam's apple in a man.

✦ This chakra rules the throat and speech organs, the mouth, the neck, the shoulders and the passages that run up to the ears.

✦ Blockages here can manifest as sore throats, swollen glands in the neck, mouth ulcers and ear problems.

✦ On a psychological level, difficulty remembering facts or dates and an inability to communicate clearly or formulate thoughts in an ordered way may result if this chakra is not working efficiently.

✦ Visualise deep sky-blue light spiralling from this chakra. Also visualise this light spiralling from the sky and into your body, even on an overcast day.

Throat chakra fragrances
✦ The main throat fragrance is lavender. Others include acacia, angelica, lily, magnolia, pine, tea tree, thyme and violet.

✦ Using a single drop of fragrance, anoint your throat.

Brow chakra
✦ The brow chakra is the chakra of light. It is situated just above the bridge of the nose, in the centre of the brow.

✦ It controls the eyes, ears, and both hemispheres of the brain, and radiates into the central cavity of the brain.

✣ Blockages here can result in blurred vision without apparent physical cause, headaches, migraines, blocked sinuses and earache.

✣ On a psychological level, insomnia or nightmares can result from malfunctions in this chakra.

✣ Picture rich turquoise or indigo/purple light emanating from this chakra. Also see this light emanating from all the crystals in and on the earth and from the angelic realms (see pages 109–19 and 128–36).

Brow chakra fragrances
✣ The main brow fragrance is papyrus flower. Others include bergamot, clary sage, lemongrass, sweet marjoram, sandalwood (second choice if papyrus is not available), sweetgrass and valerian. (Dilute lemongrass and bergamot well, 3 drops to 30 ml/2 tbsp carrier oil, as they can be skin irritants.

✣ Using a single drop of fragrance, anoint your brow.

Crown chakra
✣ The crown chakra is the chakra of unity with all things and with the source of divinity. It is situated at the top of the head, where the three main bones of the skull fuse at the anterior fontanel. It extends beyond the crown, and some locate the centre about three finger breadths above the top of the head.

✣ It rules the brain, body, mind and soul.

✣ Problems here can result in headaches, migraines and inefficient functioning of the immune system.

✣ Emotional problems manifest as difficulty integrating different aspects of the self and as a sense of alienation from the daily world.

✣ Visualise rich violet or pure white light flowing upwards from this chakra, and this light flowing downwards from the cosmos.

Crown chakra fragrances
✣ The main crown chakra fragrance is lotus. Others include ambergris, chamomile, chrysanthemum, citronella, frankincense, mandarin, rosemary (second choice), sage and sagebrush.

✣ Using a single drop of fragrance, anoint just below the centre of the hair line (if using citronella, dilute well).

Collecting chakra fragrances

In the lists above, I have suggested alternative fragrances, as some of the Egyptian ones in the original system are expensive and difficult to obtain locally. However, if you do get the chance to buy small quantities of real Egyptian essences, especially lotus and papyrus flower, take it. They are superb. Even a drop or two will demonstrate instantaneously how a pure fragrance can really lift the consciousness.

I have found lotus essential oil in the British Museum shop, and it can also be obtained from stores that sell a wide range of aromatherapy products. Papyrus flower is more difficult to obtain. You can get it by mail order via the internet and also from specialist aromatherapy outlets in other countries (for suppliers see Useful Contacts).

Fragrances for chakra work can be in the form of perfume, cologne, flower water, essential oil or incense. Yardley make an excellent selection of flower colognes including sandalwood. You can also make your own chakra essences, using the essential oil water methods described on page 41 or the flower water methods described on pages 36–8.

If you are using essential oils for anointing or massaging the chakra points, dilute a small quantity of each of your seven chosen essential oils in advance, using your favourite carrier oil. Use 7–10 drops of essential oil to 30 ml/2 tbsp of carrier oil. Be aware that some essential oils are irritants or are to be avoided in pregnancy and with certain medical conditions (see list of prohibitions on page 180). In these cases you can use the fragrances as incense or as very diluted oils. Alternatively, if your skin is sensitive or you are pregnant or chronically ill, you can apply lavender and rose water alternately on all the chakra points. These fragrances are very mild but psychically powerful.

Identifying chakra problems using a pendulum

You can identify problems with individual chakras by using a crystal pendulum. Hold the pendulum string between your thumb and the first finger of your power hand and allow it to swing freely. Alternatively, you can ask a friend or partner to run the pendulum slowly over your body (you do not need to take your clothes off).

You will feel an energetic reaction when the pendulum encounters the energy centres in your body.

Beginning at the sole of your left foot, pass the pendulum slowly upwards over the front of your body in a spiralling pattern. Continue moving upwards, via the right hand and arm, then the chest, throat and brow, remembering to hold the pendulum above the crown to fully connect with that chakra, before spiralling down the back of the body, diverting to the left arm and hand, down the back and finally to the sole of the right foot. You will reconnect with the base chakra at the small of your back.

Although they are often depicted in a straight ascending line along the spinal cord, chakras penetrate the front as well as the back of the body. Trust the pendulum to find its own pathways, as it is believed that there are thousands of tiny interconnecting psychic energy channels through the body When you reach a major chakra, the pendulum may spiral first clockwise and then anti-clockwise as it links with the vortex of energy. The sensation is rather like holding your hand over the plughole of an emptying bath. If the chakra is blocked or, conversely, over-active, the pendulum will either move sluggishly or spiral first one way then the other, totally out of control.

When you have finished, scribble a diagram to remind yourself of areas that need extra attention during your chakra cleansing and empowering. If your whole body seems sluggish or you receive a jagged metallic sensation like a mild electric shock as the pendulum traces the energy pathways, your system may be generally over-stimulated and all your chakras need attention.

Identifying chakra problems by reading your aura

The rainbow colours that I described emanating from the chakras form a swirling rainbow band around the body and especially around the head. Because this is psychic energy, most people see this only in their mind's eye.

However, it is possible actually to see your aura. To do this, sit in front of a mirror placed so that your head is framed in light (sun, moon or candle). Stare at the area around your head. Now close your eyes for a few seconds, then open them suddenly and blink and you will see the rainbow colours of your aura.

Aura reading. Page 70-71

rance of your aura, have by you a piece of
coloured pencils (containing different shades
eat the process described above a few times,
ribble a picture of your head framed by the
ntinue to alternate looking and colouring until
let your hand guide the colouring rather than
d. (You can also read someone else's aura by
by light – for example against a window or
g you. Then follow the above steps.)

all seven colours will be present, though for
orange, yellow, green and blue will be
y represent energies that are close to the
vever, as you work with fragrance magic (or,
indeed, do any other kind of spiritual work) the higher energy
centres, represented by indigo, purple and white, will open more
frequently, and these colours may eventually become equally as
clear as the others in your aura.

Dull or missing colours or harsh metallic shades in the spectrum
from red through to blue indicate imbalances. If your whole aura
is cloudy or streaked with black, you need a full chakra overhaul,
perhaps more urgently than any routine weekly or fortnightly
session you may have established.

(See page 181 for books on aura reading.)

A weekly fragrance ritual for the chakras

This ritual involves inhaling the seven chakra fragrances in turn.
If you establish it as a weekly (or fortnightly) ritual, it will help
you to feel better, happier and more able to relate to others. You
will also become more resistant to stress and pollutants.

Chakra healing is not intended as a substitute for medical advice
and treatment in acute conditions; however, in many cases I know
of personally, it has proved therapeutic, especially with chronic
problems and stress-related conditions. For example, I suffer from
gallstones, linked with the solar plexus chakra. One effect of
gallstones is that sometimes, just before an attack starts, the whole
body feels sluggish and bloated. I find that burning orange incense
will kickstart my own resistance and will often prevent the pain
from increasing.

The following ritual should be carried out in the evening, when you can be alone and quiet.

What you need: A bottle of fragrance corresponding to each chakra (see pages 64–9); a loose robe that unfastens down the front; enough candles for light to work by; 7 crystals or 7 small candles or fragrant flowers in the 7 colours of the chakras (optional).

✢ Gather together your fragrances and then have a bath, using plain water or rose bath foam. Put on your robe.

✢ Go to your indoor fragrant place and light the illumination candles. If you are using coloured crystals, candles or flowers, arrange these in a circle, lighting the candles.

✢ Use the pendulum or aura method (see pages 69–71) to ascertain where work is most needed. It is rare that there is no extra cleansing and empowering work to do, unless you live an amazingly unstressed life.

✢ If everything is fine or if your system needs energising, anoint each chakra with its fragrance, moving upwards from the base chakra to the crown. If your system needs calming, however, work downwards from the crown chakra to the base chakra. Inhale each fragrance slowly before using it and close your eyes, allowing images to form. You may also see coloured lights. Use different fingers for each fragrance, beginning with the index finger of your power hand and ending with the ring finger of the other hand (do not use your thumbs). As you work, picture the rainbow colours swirling together and merging as they move upwards to form white light and downwards to be absorbed in rich red connecting with the earth. Also visualise the natural source of each colour as listed on pages 64–9 – for example yellow sunlight enriching the solar plexus chakra.

✢ If a particular chakra is troublesome, you can massage the fragrance into the skin around the chakra area, making first anti-clockwise and then clockwise circles. This will release any tension and energise the chakra. Imagine the light of the chakra becoming clearer and the chakra swirling round more freely – as if you had removed tangled wool from a cog. This method works whatever the nature of the problem.

✢ When you have finished, put out the candles and relax.

A more complex ritual to harmonise the chakras with fragrance

What you need: Ingredients as for the Weekly Fragrance Ritual for the Chakras (see pages 71–2).

✢ Follow the steps for the Weekly Fragrance Ritual for the Chakras (see pages 71–2) but as you anoint each chakra, add a chant. The one I use was taught to me by an Egyptian woman living in London and is based on one of the old Egyptian immortality verses, 'Coming Forth by Day'. The words were originally written about the lotus. However, you can adapt the chant to apply to other chakra fragrances.

✢ As you anoint your crown chakra say:

I am the pure lotus [or name the fragrance you are using] _that comes forth from the light. I am the lotus of the shining one that comes forth from the fields of everlasting light._

Visualise pure drops of white light flowing within your body, circling around each energy centre and passing down the spiralling psychic energy channels that, it is hypothesised, criss-cross the body.

✢ Continue anointing the other chakras, imagining the colours swirling and merging and adapting the chant as necessary, for example for the brow chakra:

I am the papyrus flower that comes forth from the light ...

Other ways of working with chakra energies

There are many ways to work with chakra fragrances. With the following methods, work from crown to base or vice versa according to the guidelines in the Weekly Fragrance Ritual for the Chakras on pages 71–2, or as feels appropriate at the time.

Using fresh flowers

Find a fragrant flower in each of the chakra colours and inhale the scent of each flower in turn, naming the chakra. Keep the flowers in a vase in your indoor fragrant place. If one chakra is troublesome, sit holding the relevant flower, inhaling the scent slowly, and add more of it to the vase. Establish a gentle, regular inhale and exhale rhythm, meanwhile picturing the coloured light entering the malfunctioning chakra.

Baths

Add each of the chakra fragrances to a bath, either as a drop of perfume or as an essential oil (diluting irritants in a carrier oil before using them). As you add each one, say:

Fragrance flow free, release from me negativity, leaving only harmony.

Use additional drops of fragrance for any troublesome chakras.

Oils

Drop each of the chakra oils, as a single drop, into a lit oil burner, as you do so repeating the lotus and other fragrance chants given on page 73. Use additional drops of oil for any troublesome chakras.

Scented candles

In fireproof holders, make a circle of small squat candles scented with the chakra fragrances. Sit in the centre of the circle and, as you inhale the fragrance, imagine the perfumed smoke cleansing and empowering you. Allow the candles to burn down.

Smudging

This method should be worked outdoors. Light a sagebrush smudge stick or firm sage incense stick, but rather than fanning it, move the stick upwards from your feet, smudging each in turn and moving from the left to the right diagonally so that you set up a rhythm. Keep the smoking end of the smudge a few centimetres from your body and waft it alternately anti-clockwise to cleanse and then clockwise to empower. Pause at each chakra centre, making two anti-clockwise and then two clockwise smoke circles over the chakra area, taking more time over any troublesome chakra. Smudge your hands and arms, this time the right first and then the left. When you reach the crown chakra, make an anti-clockwise and then a clockwise circle, followed by a second clockwise circle above your head. Then repeat the smudge downwards to your feet. If you wish you can chant softly as you smudge:

Above to the ground, peace surround.

It is also possible for two people to smudge each other – as though they are dancing.

CHAPTER 6
Fragrant Dreams

Adults and children alike can suffer from insomnia and nightmares. The frantic pace of the modern world means that all too often we go to bed with our heads whirling, full of lists of unfinished chores and anticipation of the day ahead. Late-night television and computer games can further over-stimulate the mind. The transition from waking to sleep, marked in pre-television days by cocoa round the fire and quiet conversation, is now often a final frantic dash to get everything completed before we collapse into bed.

Fragrances, whether used in baths, as sleep pillows or as scented candles, are a natural way to restore the gentle transition time into sleep. They can also help us to find answers to problems or questions in our dreams – as people have done for thousands of years – by creating an aromatic pathway into the world of unconscious knowledge.

Fragrant baths

Long before commercial herbal bath preparations were invented or, indeed, bathrooms became common in ordinary homes, men and women would add herbs, lavender heads or rose petals to the tub to bring quiet sleep, or place chamomile in a fractious child's bath.

Modern plumbing means that you cannot add your herbs or petals directly to the bath without clogging up the pipes. But there are still ways you can enjoy the floral and herbal mixes tried and loved by our ancestors. Supermarkets, pharmacies, and health and beauty stores have a huge range of herbal and floral bath products. If you read the labels, you will find that a number contain only natural products.

If you are busy, ready-made bath essences mean that you can instantly release the power inherent in the scents – and the rituals

I suggest work well whether the bath products you use are home-made or shop-bought. The other advantage of buying bath foams and oils is that good-quality hypo-allergenic or non-chemical products will not irritate even delicate skin as they are carefully tested, some brands without using animals.

You may also find lovely bath products at school and church fetes, farmers' markets, country fairs and town or city markets where stall holders come from miles around. My own favourite is the Sunday market in Rouen in France, where there is stall after stall selling wonderful fresh herbs and flowers from the garden as well as bath products prepared according to old family recipes. My favourite is an acacia and honey mix, the original tree cutting brought back to France from India in the 1930s. (My local supermarket on the Isle of Wight, it has to be said, does a version that is almost as soothing.)

A relaxing fragrant bath

If you have had a stressful or frantic day or you just want some 'own' time, make your pre-sleep bath a special occasion, undisturbed by phone calls, family demands and noise.

✢ Lock the door so no one can pop into the bathroom to chat, moan, comment on your cellulite, ask to borrow money for a night out or suggest they share your bath – whether toddler, the dog or amorous lover.

✢ Light small candles scented with rose, ylang ylang, peach or orange in safe places around the bathroom.

✢ Make sure the bathroom is warm and that there are plenty of fluffy towels and your bathrobe is ready.

✢ Play gentle dolphin or ocean music on a waterproof battery-operated CD player.

✢ Add fragrant herbs, foam, oils or salts to your bath.

✢ When the bath is ready, lie in the water, swirling the fragrant pools of light and symbolically pushing away in them any worries or negativity left from the day.

✢ Through half-closed eyes allow the light and patterns of foam or oils on the surface of the water to make beautiful images. Let these pictures flow in and out of your mind without analysing them and then push away even these pleasant images, finally emptying your mind of all but the beautiful fragrance, the music and the candle light.

✣ When you are ready, get out of the bath and wrap yourself in warm towels, pulling out the plug and allowing the water to run away, and saying softly:

Sorrow and stress, flow from me, to the rivers and the sea, leaving only harmony.

Pour a few drops of pine or tea tree essential oil down the plughole to make sure only positive energies remain.

✣ Blow out each of the candles one by one, either making a wish for each or sending blessings or healing to someone or somewhere that needs it. Leave the last candle alight and carefully carry it to your bedroom.

✣ Do not read or watch television in bed but sit quietly gazing into the fragrant candle flame, allowing pictures and stories to come, perhaps ones you saw in your bath, that will lead you into your dreams. If you share your bed, talk softly to your sleep companion, about something other than domestic or work concerns, carrying him or her into your quiet world between waking and sleep.

✣ Finally blow out the candle and ask that the light protect you, your family and your home while you sleep.

Herbal bath sachets

Making herbal bath sachets is a very soothing activity, and family members can join in with the preparation and mixing of the herbs. In the past these making and talking sessions helped to harmonise relationships between different generations living in close proximity. If you ask your grandmother, your mother or one of your older in-laws, they may well recall herbal recipes from their childhood, and this shared recollection can also help to establish bonds of affection. Talking about the different properties of the herbs and flowers creates a quiet space for people to share their worries, fears, hopes and dreams or just to be together in companionable silence.

But even working alone you can tap into the shared experiences of women who throughout the ages gathered and prepared fragrant herbs. And if you write your favourite recipes in your journal you can pass on your insights to future generations.

The following herbs and flowers are especially good for inducing relaxation and peaceful sleep:

+ Chamomile flowers
+ Carnation petals
+ Catnip (small quantity only)
+ Elecampane
+ Elderflower
+ Eucalyptus (surprisingly relaxing)
+ Fennel seeds
+ Jasmine flowers
+ Hop flowers
+ Hyssop
+ Lavender
+ Lemon verbena
+ Lilac
+ Linden blossoms
+ Marjoram (sweet)
+ Melissa (lemon balm)
+ Olive blossoms
+ Orange peel (dried)
+ Orange blossom (neroli)
+ Passionflower
+ Peppermint
+ Rosemary
+ Rose petals

✤ Skullcap leaves

✤ Slippery elm bark

✤ Valerian root

These are just some suggestions and you can add your own favourite flowers and herbs as long as they are not toxic. If in doubt check in a herb book (see page 182). Commercially prepared mixtures tend to be a good guide to what works. Indeed, before making your own you might like to buy some manufactured herbal bath sachets consisting of natural ingredients to see which fragrances suit you best.

Making herbal bath sachets

You can use herbs and flowers from the garden for your sachets as long as you garden organically. Alternatively, you can buy freshly picked organic flowers (some garden centres and florists stock these) or organic pot herbs, stocked by some supermarkets. Many dried culinary herbs are excellent in baths and you can also use dried flower petals and powdered roots, available from healthfood shops and old-fashioned grocers. The same box of chamomile from which you make tea can also serve as a soothing bath. You can use a single type of herb or flower for your sachets or mix them. If you experiment with different combinations, don't forget to make a note of your favourites.

What you need: Fresh herbs and flowers of your choice (washed and chopped); pieces of muslin, cheesecloth or similar porous material cut to about 15 × 20 cm (7 × 8 in) or alternatively pieces cut from the leg of a pair of tights or a stocking, or any kind of small net bag whose colour will not run (for example the meshed nets put on soft fruits); string or cord (unless you are making your bags from tights or stockings).

✤ If you are using cloth, fold each piece in half across its width and sew three sides in running stitch to make the bag, picturing light and peace entering every stitch as you do so. If you are using tights, knot one end.

✤ Fill the bags (or tights or nets or whatever you are using) with the flowers and herbs. As you do this, state the purpose for which you are making the sachet. For example:

*I ask that the jasmine flowers and orange blossom petals in
this sachet will bring my daughter Melody quiet sleep and
peaceful dreams that she may wake refreshed and able to
cope with her examination tomorrow.*

✢ Tie the tops of the bags with string or cord, or knot the tights. For
each knot make a wish or empowerment concerning the purpose
of the herbs, such as:

*One knot that Melody will have faith in herself, two that she
may not panic, three that she will draw on the love of the
family for support and not shut herself away with her worries.*

✢ Use the sachets as soon as possible, as they lose their fragrance
quickly. If you do need to store them, use airtight jars and keep the
storage time to a minimum.

Using the sachets

✢ Run your bath, making sure the water is warm but not hot –
around 36 °C/98 °F, just below body temperature. Anything hotter
will exhaust you and anything cooler will be too stimulating.

✢ Place the bath sachet in the bottom of the bath. Don't get in until
it has been infusing in the water for five minutes; then, get into the
bath, leaving the bath sachet in the water with you for a further
five minutes. When the five minutes are up, squeeze the last of the
infusion out of the sachet and remove it from the bath.

✢ Alternatively, hang the bath sachet just below the tap as you run
your bath, allowing the water to run through it.

Making herbal infusions for the bath

If you prefer, you can make a herbal infusion or decoction and add
it to the bath water. (You can also use fragrant herbal infusions for
protective floor washes or to sprinkle in rooms that seem
unfriendly or dark.)

What you need: 50 g/2 oz fresh herbs or flowers (washed), or 40 g/
1½ oz dried herbs; 600 ml/1 pint/2½ cups boiling water; a bowl or
jug; dark glass bottles with a screw-top lid or cork (if the infusion
is to be stored).

✢ Place the herbs or flowers in the bowl or jug and add the boiling
water. This infusion is slightly stronger than the kind you use for

teas. For children and people with delicate skins use a weaker infusion, halving the quantity of herbs above.

✤ Stir the infusion, as you do so naming the herbs or flowers and their purpose, for example:

Lavender, bring me dreams of love and fertility that I may rise above my present loneliness.

✤ Cover the infusion and leave it to stand for about 10 minutes, stirring occasionally and repeating the chant. If the matter is important, enchant the infusion (see pages 31–2).

✤ When 10 minutes has elapsed, strain the infusion, discard the herbs and petals, and either pour the infusion into the bath or store it in the dark glass bottles. It will keep in the fridge for about a week.

Making a bath decoction

A decoction is a method of extracting the essence from roots and barks. Roots should be powdered, crushed in a pestle, finely chopped or bought ready-chopped. This preparation provides a chance to declare the purpose of the decoction in a slow repetitive chant. For example:

Valerian, valerian, bring sleep to my sister Mary, who lies awake every night worrying needlessly.

If you buy your roots pre-prepared, you can still mix them and chant.

What you need: 25 g/1 oz roots (powdered, crushed or finely chopped) and barks; 600 ml/1 pint/2½ cups cold water; a ceramic saucepan; dark glass bottles with a screw-top lid or cork (if the infusion is to be stored).

✤ Place the roots and barks in the saucepan and add the water. Simmer the mixture until the water is reduced by half.

✤ Strain the mixture, squeezing the roots and barks to get all the liquid out. Discard the herbs.

✤ Either pour the infusion into the bath or store it in the dark glass bottles. It will keep in the fridge for about a week.

Oil dream baths

Another option is to add 10 drops of essential oil to the bath after running it. Use only 3–5 drops of citrus oils such as orange and potent oils such as peppermint. Try using the oil versions of some of the flowers and herbs I have suggested above. In addition, clary sage, mimosa, rosewood and sandalwood are very soothing sleep oils and are most often found in essential oil form. If you want to experiment, check the table of correspondences on pages 171–80.

Dream pillows

Sleeping on a dream pillow is a traditional way of inducing peaceful sleep and happy dreams. Dream pillows are small, cushion-sized pillows filled with fragrant herbs that calm and relax. They are still sold at country fairs and in rural gift stores. In the modern world they have even appeared in microwaveable form.

Children who suffer from night terrors, nightmares or fears of the dark may benefit from one of the commercially available dream pillows in the form of a lavender- or rose-filled bear. If you are good at sewing you can make your own, with an inner herb-filled pillow. For children chamomile, lavender and rose petals are the best herbs to use, as they are very mild. Make sure the child cannot open the cover and chew the herbs.

Dried herbs and flower petals are the best choice for dream pillows. You can use any of the herbs or flowers listed on pages 78–9 as suitable for bath sachets; however, the following herbs are especially associated with pleasant dreams:

+ **Angelica** is good for out-of-body and healing dreams.

+ **Anise** keeps away nightmares. (Use very small quantities.)

+ **Chamomile** brings quiet sleep when you are exhausted or over-anxious. This is the best herb for curing insomnia.

+ **Cloves** (again, use just a few) bring dreams of childhood and of old friends and family members who are absent or who have died.

+ **Hops** bring peaceful sleep. They are not very fragrant, so combine them with other ingredients.

+ **Lavender** brings gentle dreams of love or of the future.

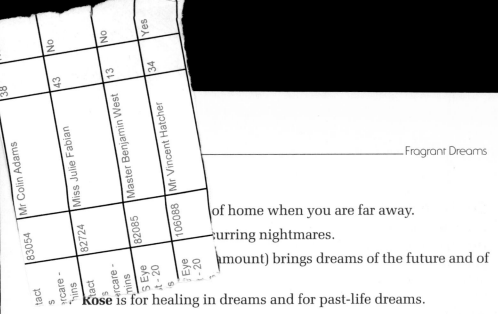

... of home when you are far away.

... ...urring nightmares.

... ...mount) brings dreams of the future and of

Rose is for healing in dreams and for past-life dreams.

✦ **Rosemary** (in small quantities so as not to overwhelm other fragrances) drives away night terrors and defuses fears of the dark or of sleeping alone – at any age.

✦ **St John's wort** brings dreams of future marriages or long-lasting love and takes away grief while you sleep.

✦ **Sweet marjoram** brings happy dreams when life is sad.

✦ **Valerian** brings gentle dreams and banishes insomnia.

The following oils are also associated with dreams. Add a drop or two to your sleep pillow herbs to increase the fragrance, but do not use in children's pillows.

✦ **Frankincense** brings dreams of magical places and ancient ceremonies.

✦ **Myrrh** brings past-life memories and healing dreams.

✦ **Orange** brings dreams of happy relationships and banishes the regrets of the day.

✦ **Sandalwood** brings dreams of passion and of past lives.

✦ **Ylang ylang** brings dreams of love and psychic dreams.

Making a Dream Pillow

Dream pillows are very easy to make. However, if you are short of time you can buy two cushion covers, one larger and one smaller, with zips or Velcro fastening. Fill the smaller cushion with your herbs or flowers and put it inside the larger one. Buy a really cheap inner cover as they are seldom worth refilling, and throwing them away is better from a psychic point of view. Car boot sales are a good source of old pillows and cushions from which you can cannibalise the covers.

If you are using ready-made cushion covers, empower them before use by setting them near the herbs that they are to contain and

Dream Pillows

lighting a fragrant yellow, pink or lilac candle. Then place them in a pool of sunlight or moonlight. You can empower them further before you fill them by holding them and visualising fields of flowers in which you drift gently into sleep.

What you need: A piece of thin natural fabric, such as cotton, large enough to make a pillow about 15 cm/6 in square; a piece of muslin, mesh or fine net curtain cut to about 13 cm/5 in square; a glass or ceramic bowl; a wooden or ceramic spoon; an essential oil of your choice (omit if the pillow is for a child); Velcro to close the cushions (optional)

✣ Decide which herbs and flowers you are going to use by experimenting with different mixes in the bowl. When you are satisfied, set the chosen flowers and/or herbs in the bowl so that you can inhale the aroma as you work.

✣ Stitch up the sides of the fabric for the outer pillow, leaving the top open. Work either in sunlight or by moonlight or candlelight, and as you sew, picture light entering the stitches. Visualise whoever you are making the pillow for (maybe yourself) in a field filled with the herbs and flowers, falling asleep on a bed of fragrance.

✣ Stitch up the sides of the muslin, mesh or net for the inner pillow.

✣ Begin to mix the herbs and flowers with a wooden or ceramic spoon (even if you are using a single flower or herb). Add two or three drops of your chosen essential oil. Do not chant but work in silence, imagining light continuing to pour into the bowl. The light may take on the colour of the plants or flowers you are mixing. You will sense when the herbs are ready (you may detect, or see in your mind's eye, a faint aura of light around the bowl).

✣ At this point hold your hands, palms downwards, over the bowl, but do not move them. Your fingers will vibrate slightly. Whisper softly:

> *May sleep come swiftly and gently. May Mother Night carry you/me into sweet dreams. May angels keep away all harm and fear, and in the morning may you/I with joy and renewal wake restored.*

✣ Fill the inner pillow with herbs, stuffing it loosely enough for the herbs to be able to move around, and then sew it closed or sew on Velcro fastenings.

✣ Slip the herbal pillow into the outer cover. Sew up the outer cover or sew on Velcro fastenings and leave the completed pillow in any remaining sun, moon or candlelight until the light is gone or the candle is burnt through.

✣ When the herbs lose their fragrance, tip them out and scatter them to the winds or you can bury them beneath a fruit- or nut-bearing tree.

Fragrant candles for peaceful sleep

One of the most effective ways to drive away fears and ensure quiet sleep is to light a scented night-light or small aromatic candle. If you use a deep glass container with coloured sand inside, the candle will be safe even if you drift off to sleep, although it is better to extinguish the candle.

Insomniac or frightened children will benefit from a candle fragranced with apple blossom, chamomile, jasmine, lavender, mimosa, rose, sandalwood or ylang ylang burned in the bedroom before sleep. This is much gentler than incense and safer than burning oils. If the child is willing, you can invite them to visualise the light of the candle by closing their eyes and imagining seeing the burning candle in darkness. Then, when the room is fragranced, you can blow out the candle together and ask the child to lie down with their eyes closed, still picturing the light, as the fragrance lingers.

An alternative for a child who is frightened of the dark is to light five small scented night-lights. Blow out the night-lights one at a time, but tell the child to sit with their eyes open and picture the extinguished light as if it was still burning. Describe the extinguished light as a fragrance fairy or angel who will shine a magical protective light all night. As the room gets gradually darker, the child will still be able to 'see' the five light fairies and can call on them on waking at any time during the night.

Creating meaningful dreams with fragrance

The following method for creating or incubating dreams can be practised nightly for a week and thereafter whenever needed. It will often spontaneously provide answers to questions that trouble you, and if you have no specific questions it will create a beautiful sleep experience from which you will awake relaxed and refreshed. It will also rapidly harmonise sleep patterns if you are an insomniac and will help you to rest if you have experienced a particularly pressurised few weeks.

What you need: Scented bath/shower products of your choice; night-lights to illuminate the bathroom; some gentle music; a small candle or night-light for the bedroom; rose or lavender essential oil, or cologne, or your favourite gentle fragrance.

✣ Set the phone to silent answer, switch off the fax machine and do not check your e-mails just before getting ready for bed – it is all too easy to slip back into social or work mode.

✣ Have a scented bath or shower, using the night-lights to illuminate the bathroom.

✣ Afterwards, when you are in your night clothes in your bedroom, have a herbal or milky drink while you sit in semi-darkness listening to the music.

✣ When you are totally relaxed, light the small candle or night-light. Put it in a safe place in your bedroom and sit on the bed facing it, well propped up on pillows.

✣ In the candlelight, gently smell the fragrance you have chosen. Imagine yourself in a beautiful rose garden or field of lavender or some other flowery place.

✣ Sprinkle just a drop or two of the fragrance on your pillow to transfer the scent experience to the realms of sleep.

✣ Blow out the candle and close your eyes, in your imagination stepping through the flowers, field upon field, until at last you sink down among the fragrant blossoms into the world of dreams.

Creating psychic dreams

What you need: Scented bath/shower products of your choice; night-lights to illuminate the bathroom; some gentle music; a small candle or night-light, scented with sandalwood, frankincense or myrrh for the bedroom.

✛ Follow the method on page 86 until the point where you light your candle. This time, as you light the sandalwood-, frankincense- or myrrh-scented candle, allow a question to form quite spontaneously in your mind. The choice may surprise you.

✛ Repeat this question in your head more and more slowly until your inner voice becomes silent.

✛ Blow out the candle and allow the lingering fragrance to continue working as, once more repeating the question over and over again, you drift into sleep. Your dreams will contain scenes or symbols that will fill your mind with optimism, ideas for creative opportunities, or solutions to problems when you wake. If you are in doubt about the meaning of your dream, smell the fragrance again – it will give you the key.

CHAPTER 7
Fragrance and Spiritual Development

Perfumes, oils and incenses quite spontaneously open pathways to higher states of awareness, whether in the form of meditation or of visualisation – the psychic art of focusing the imagination on a desired event or object. Fragrances also open doors to past worlds and to mind travel, in which, when very relaxed, you may feel as if you are leaving your body and travelling to other lands or even to what seem to be mythological settings. It is on these aspects of psychic development that we will be focusing in this chapter.

We all have innate, natural psychic powers that enable us to glimpse beyond the here and now. These are manifest in daily life as intuition – the instinctive awareness that if trusted can accurately guide us to make wise decisions even when we may not have all the facts. The problem is getting beyond the blocks put by the conscious mind on this instinctive sense. Fragrance is a particularly good tool for loosening the tight boundaries of what can be explained logically (and which is usually only half the picture). In Chapter 1 we worked with clairsentience, psychic sensing using aromas. That quite natural ability forms the cornerstone of the experiences we will be exploring in this chapter.

I have used the terms 'psychic' and 'spiritual' interchangeably. Sometimes 'psychic' is used to refer to personal powers and 'spiritual' to refer to connections with higher energies such as angels or higher intentions such as healing. However, I would argue that any psychic work, if carried out with a will to good and a pure heart, is by its nature spiritual.

Fragrant pathways to understanding

Fragrances have always been prized as gateways to other dimensions in which we can connect with the higher wisdom that earlier civilisations considered to be the gods themselves speaking to mortals.

When I went to Egypt I was determined to track down the famous lotus essence reputed to be one of the quickest and most powerful keys to unlocking psychic powers, not only in Egypt but also in other lands, such as India, where the lotus is native. I discovered more in Cairo Museum, which holds the earliest known statue of the lotus god, found in the entrance to the tomb of Tutankhamun. It depicts the boy King as Nefertum, the lotus god, rising from the first lotus at the first sunrise on the day of creation, and it is exquisite and beautifully coloured. The fragrant blue lotus (a form of water lily) opens at dawn, and so came to symbolise the first and every subsequent sunrise. The equally fragrant white lotus, also used in perfume-making, opens in the evening.

Although I was aware of the divine reputation of the lotus, when I inhaled a glass stopper steeped in the pure lotus essence in an Egyptian perfume store, I was totally overwhelmed by the instant psychic effects of the fragrance on me. Suddenly I had a sense of being in a past world, in one of the old tombs at a funeral. I was very old and knew that I would soon be buried myself. I became aware that this was the burial of my husband. In this past-life world we had been together for many years and the lotus was our flower. I was not afraid and was glad his spirit would be waiting for mine in the Field of Reeds, where the fortunate dead lived on the banks of the celestial river of stars, the Milky Way. I was filled with a sense of overwhelming peace as light flooded from the flowers in the darkened tomb, and I promised to bring lotus flowers every day to his offerings temple.

While the powers of lotus are pretty spectacular, there are many other fragrances that evoke our innate psychism. Some are exotic ceremonial aromas such as frankincense, myrrh and sandalwood; others are the natural scents of gardens and woodland. It would seem that some fragrances are like computer zip files that open pathways to our psychic senses. Whatever form of psychic work you are undertaking, you can use fragrances in a variety of ways to help you access the richness of your unconscious mind.

Even if you do not accept the idea of innate psychic abilities, the unconscious does hold all kinds of stored information that we have forgotten we know, beginning with experiences from our earliest childhood. This knowledge is often received in symbolic form at times when our bodies and minds are relaxed. If we take time to unravel these images, we may gain a new perspective on current issues in our lives.

Fragrant forms for unlocking your psychic senses

Over time you will develop your own favourite ways of using fragrance to develop your psychic ability. The following are some of the most effective methods of using different forms of fragrance.

Incense

Although there are other forms of incense, incense sticks have the advantage that they can be used with no preparation and the effect is instant. Most incense sticks will last for about half an hour, which is plenty of time for most psychic explorations. If you want to work for longer, some of the better quality sticks will burn for up to an hour. You can mix the fragrances by lighting two or three differently scented sticks at once.

Experiment with floral and fruit incenses as well as the ceremonial types, such as frankincense, myrrh and sandalwood. Even plants with little natural fragrance, such as fern and ivy, are highly aromatic as incense. If there is a chance that you may drift off to sleep (as sometimes happens during meditation), burn your incense sticks in a deep container on a metal tray to catch hot ash. Also have in the room a dish of water for extinguishing sticks (by plunging them into the water) or (the older method) a pot filled with sand or earth.

Aromatic oils

Essential oils or the less pure but more varied fragrance oils can be burned to enhance meditation or visualisation work, as well as prior to psychic work, ritual or healing. Fragrance oils are obtained not by distillation but generally by adding the fragrance in a liquid form. They are therefore not as strong or as therapeutic as essential oils and should not be used as perfume or in baths. Refresher oils for pot pourri are categorised as fragrance oils.

An oil burner and essential oil gives the purest aroma. Choose a burner with a deep bowl on top for the oil. I find metal ones the best. To use the burner, half fill the bowl with water and add a few drops of essential oil. Some people microwave the water for a minute before putting it in the burner. This enables the quicker release of fragrance and some say it produces a purer scent. Fragrance oils are already diluted and need little if any water. Next light a tea-light beneath the bowl. This is much safer than using a small candle, which creates too intense a heat. If you want to combine the properties of different aromas, you can burn more than one essential oil at once. You can also increase the intensity of the fragrance by adding more drops of oil.

To top up the burner, add warm water and then a drop or two more of oil if the fragrance is fading. You can end a ritual by carefully blowing out the night-light. For greater safety, use a metal candle snuffer. The oil and water remains hot for some time, which gives the advantage that the residual fragrance provides an easy transition between psychic work and sleep or a gentle return to the everyday world.

You can also buy electric oil diffusers, which are safe and easy to use but not as magical as the traditional kind. Another alternative is to drop oil into a bowl of steaming water, although the fragrance will not be as long-lasting.

Scented candles

Candles are best for visualisation work and for meditation if you are new to it, as they provide a tangible centre on which to focus. They can also be used to create an imaginary doorway of light for past-life and out-of-body mind travel.

Candles have the advantage of being long-lasting while at the same time you can instantly extinguish them when you need to in ritual or psychic work, sending the light to yourself or whoever needs it. Some candles have a maximum burning time stated on the label.

My preferred candles for psychic work, especially when it involves past lives, are beeswax, perhaps the oldest form of candle and one that is subtly aromatic. Beeswax candles are fast-burning and their wax tends to spread quite a long way, so place a metal tray beneath them if they are in an open holder.

Candles do require great care and should be kept away from animals and children, except under close supervision. If you are doing work where you are in a very relaxed state or may drift off to sleep, you can make candles safer by using a deep glass container and putting coloured sand in the bottom.

For more evolved work, such as astral travel (see pages 98–100), you may find it best to use both incense and candles.

Perfume

You can also inhale essential oils, colognes and flower waters to unlock your psychic senses (as you did for inducing beautiful dreams – see page 86). Traditional single fragrances that have been used for hundreds or even thousands of years work better than modern synthetic blends. Rose, lavender or jasmine inhaled from a glass stopper or from the bottle are effective for most kinds of psychic work.

Natural aromas

My own most powerful stimulus for spiritual explorations is the aroma of the natural world, and at times when your indoor or outdoor place is especially fragrant you may not need any artificially induced aromas to enter a meditative state or visualise clearly a desired goal.

I once had a wonderful, though brief, spontaneous meditation beneath an orange tree in full blossom within the garden of the fortified church at Almería in Andalusia. I went back another day and sat beneath the lemon tree in the garden and saw completely different images. Chapter 1 discussed clairsentience (see pages 20–3), psychic sensing using natural aromas. You may already have experienced quite vivid images as you worked with herbs and flowers for other purposes.

Finding your soul fragrance

While different scents have an affinity with different forms of psychic exploration, at the same time, just as we each have our own signature fragrance, we each tend to have one specific fragrance that transports us to deeper levels of awareness most easily. This fragrance will provide the most vivid images and emotions whether we are gazing into a candle flame to still our mind or walking through an imaginary light doorway to seek an ancient civilisation with which we feel instinctive kinship.

This soul fragrance may be the same as your signature perfume, in which case you can apply it before meditation or use it as soap or bath gel as you soak in a hot tub to distance yourself from the pressures of the day and prepare yourself for psychic work. More usually, however, this special fragrance is a single floral scent such as acacia, carnation, hyacinth, jasmine, lavender or rose, or one of the wood aromas such as cedarwood, rosewood or sandalwood.

You will generally know instinctively when you find your soul fragrance. If in doubt, set a number of your favourite single scents or oils in a circle and ask your pendulum to pull down over your soul fragrance. (For more information on how to use a pendulum, see page 128.)

Before any spiritual work, use a single drop of your soul fragrance to anoint yourself in the centre of your brow. This place is known as the third eye and is also the brow chakra point, which traditionally opens the channels of spiritual awareness. As you anoint, ask that you will work for the highest good and with the purest intentions.

Other ways to use your soul fragrance in psychic work are to burn it as a single incense stick or to add 5–6 drops of it to a bowl of boiling water set in the room in which you are working.

Meditation

Even for beginners, meditation is one of the easiest ways to shut out the clutter of the conscious mind. If you have ever sat by a pool or fountain, or on a beach trickling sand through your fingers, you have spontaneously entered a meditative state in which seconds seem hours and the everyday world melted away in the sound of the water.

Meditation has been described as the pause between two thoughts or the silence between two waves. It is essentially a state of being and existing rather than doing and reacting, an alien concept in the modern frantic world. From this state of being many deep personal insights come. Meditation is not only valuable in itself but can also lead to other psychic pathways, such as those into past worlds.

Fragrance is a powerful tool in meditation and there are various ways of using it. You can focus on the aura around a scented candle flame or on incense smoke and be carried into a meditative state by the power of the perfume. Alternatively, you can focus on a fragrant plant and merge with its essence rather than observing it, using its perfume to carry you beyond the rigid boundaries of the self and into something greater.

Good fragrances for meditation include carnation, frankincense, jasmine, lavender, melissa (lemon balm), mimosa, musk (synthetic), orange, myrrh, rosewood, sandalwood, sweet marjoram and ylang ylang.

Basic fragrance meditation

Work after dusk or in the early morning in your indoor or outdoor fragrant place. Before you start the exercise, choose a fragrant object to focus on. This could be a scented candle or the smoke from incense sticks entwining as it rises. You could also focus on a fragrant tree or a bank of scented flowers in the garden, or a vase of flowers or a large potted herb indoors. If you are new to meditation or are feeling stressed, it may also be helpful to play soft music, for example pan pipes, harp music or synthesised pieces with natural sounds running through the melody.

What you need: A fragrant plant or object of your choice to meditate on (see above).

✢ Sit or lie in any position in which you are comfortable and can see the object you are focusing on without straining your neck. Though a cross-legged position on the floor with a straight back, chin dropped slightly forward and palms uppermost is recommended, it is no good attempting to force yourself into a perfect lotus position if your knees are protesting or your back is aching while your mind is trying to float off.

✢ Focus through half-closed eyes on whatever you have chosen. Feel free to blink or even close your eyes momentarily.

✣ Maintaining the focus, begin to notice your breath. Establish a rhythm, taking a slow, deep breath in through your nose to the count of three and inhaling the fragrance. Hold your breath for three and then exhale for three. Then pause for three before inhaling again. If you find that counting distracts you, simply concentrate on creating a regular pattern so that you merge with the fragrance and feel yourself enclosed by the petals or the branches, or able to step mentally into the light or smoke halo.

✣ Visualise yourself as part of the fragrance, flowing upwards and around. If you are using candlelight, allow the patterns of the candle flame to create swirling roadways along which the fragrance travels. If you are concentrating on a flower or tree, picture gold or green beams of light spiralling upwards from it and the fragrance expanding as you breathe so that you are enclosed in fragrant light.

✣ As you are temporarily freed from the restrictions of your physical body, you may find yourself travelling in your mind to other places in the world, to the past or the future, or to the realms of myth. You may hear words or see images, or you may just experience a sense of peace and connection with life and nature – this is no less worthwhile than specific pictures or mind travel.

✣ After a while you will become aware of the sounds of the physical world again. Sit or lie quietly for a few minutes enjoying the fragrance and letting your mind process the experience in its own way. If possible, don't rush straight back into life; however, if you do need to plunge back into earthly demands, you will be calmer. You may find that your dreams that night are peaceful and filled with rich symbols.

Fragrance meditation for the more experienced

As you gain experience in meditation, try working with incense sticks in a single fragrance in the following way.

What you need: Incense sticks in a single fragrance.

✣ Light the incense, get comfortable, close your eyes and picture the plant from which the incense was made. Gradually begin to imagine yourself becoming part of the plant. Feel it expand to encompass you. Let your breathing be in time with the plant's, so that as it exhales oxygen, you inhale it.

✣ Allow your meditation to unfold, remaining with it until it comes to a natural end.

Visualisation

Visualisation is a more active form of meditation and is routinely practised by children when they are wishing intensely for something they want more than anything in the world. It is also the basis of many folk love rituals of the kind in which a young girl brushes her hair a hundred times while looking into a mirror by moonlight or candlelight and calling the name of her love or asking a lover yet unknown to appear in the glass. In some of these rituals the girl holds a rose or another fragrant herb, using the scent to call her lover. (See pages 162–4 for similar spells.)

There is nothing selfish in visualising what you need for yourself. If you are worried about how you are going to keep the car on the road or pay for a child's school trip, even the most powerful aroma will probably fail to carry you to spiritual realms until you have sorted out the immediate problem. Visualising yourself, for example, getting a job you really want or passing your driving test is a powerful tool for increasing the confidence that enables you to deal with the real situation positively and win through. You can also visualise healing coming to a sick friend or peace coming to a war-torn area.

Good visualisation fragrances include apple blossom, cedarwood, coconut, frankincense, hibiscus, lemongrass, orange, peach, sandalwood, strawberry and vanilla.

How visualisation works

An aroma such as the fragrant smoke of a scented candle, perhaps with a slight breeze to make the flame dance, can help you to get beyond your immediate doubts and anxieties and tap into possibilities and potential for attracting what you need. Visualisations work less well with a natural source of fragrance such as flowers or with incense unless you are an experienced visualiser, as they do not provide the same backdrop as the candle flame for imaging.

Scientists are increasingly recognising that everything in our world is made up of moving energy. Therefore it may be possible to produce what we need simply by concentrating on it. This technique is called psychokinesis (meaning 'mind power'). Assisted by the potency of a psychically effective aroma, you could draw to yourself, not the Lottery jackpot (that is a want, not a need) but, for example, a printer that someone is getting rid of when yours has broken down. Or you might get off the bus a stop early on what seems like impulse and go past a shop having a closing-down sale with a printer going for a quarter of the normal price. Of course, you might have met that friend of a friend who eventually offered you the printer free anyway, and you might have got off the bus a stop early in any case, but after visualisation you are more likely to go to the right place at the right time.

Basic fragrance visualisation

Visualisation is best practised either in the early morning or just before bed. You can repeat it nightly if necessary, using the same fragrance.

What you need: A scented candle.

✢ Light the scented candle and follow the movement of the flame with your eyes before you begin the visualisation.

✢ Establish a regular breathing pattern as described on page 95, but this time hold your hands out, palms facing upwards.

✢ Using your mind's eye (no different from imagination), picture whatever it is that you need – for example you passing an examination – as an image surrounding the candle flame. Imagine the textures, sounds, colours and any aromas.

✢ Now, slowly and regularly breathing the fragrance in and out, on each in-breath draw the image in the candle flame towards your outstretched hands. Let it become larger and more three-dimensional. Continue to increase the size and clarity of the image as you go on breathing, until eventually it fills your field of vision.

✢ When you feel as if you can touch the image or almost step into the scene, on a sudden loud out-breath imagine an equally sudden explosion of light from the candle flame, as though you are capturing the image with a flash-camera or an x-ray machine.

✦ When you can feel the excitement of the moment that you attain your goal or the healing reaches the person who needs it, blow out the candle but continue to hold the image in your mind.

✦ If it is morning, go out with your new confidence and make plans or allow your intuition to guide you to the right place and person. If it is evening, go quietly to bed – your dreams may be filled with ideas about how you can manifest your need in your daily life.

Astral travel

The word astral means 'star', and travelling to other dimensions through the skies is a way of describing our freedom from material concerns and limitations when we can step beyond the confines of our body.

The idea of leaving your body and travelling to other places, whether in dreams or while awake, can seem alarming. In fact it is estimated that more than a third of people in the Western world have had at least one spontaneous out-of-body experience, in which they appear to float above their body, their spirit self travelling to other places in the world or even to mythological realms. You may already have experienced the out-of-body sensation of floating while meditating, and you may have seen in that moment that seemed to last for hours a place in history or that seemed to come from fairy stories.

The mind traveller can bring the travelling spirit back to its body at any time by counting backwards from ten to nought. Alternatively, the experience will end naturally when a sudden noise or a demand from daily life intrudes. So astral travel is perfectly safe and you can't lose your body or the way back, because part of your mind is still focused on the real world while the other part goes walkabout (if you like, in an extended form of daydreaming).

A number of writers and researchers, myself included, do not believe that in astral travel you literally float away from your body in a spirit form but rather that the mind can travel to different dimensions while the body is in a relaxed state.

One difference between astral travel and meditation is that in astral travel you deliberately focus on obtaining this kind of travelling experience, whereas in meditation you are led there spontaneously – or not. You can also decide in advance where you wish to travel astrally and direct the experience accordingly.

Good fragrances for astral travel include basil, carnation, cedarwood, copal, frankincense, hibiscus, mint, rosemary, rosewood, pine, sage, sandalwood, sweet marjoram and thyme.

Inducing astral travel with fragrance

As I mentioned earlier in the chapter, fragrance forms a natural doorway to other realms. For this exercise we use a scented candle as the entry point, although you might also like to burn incense or add essential oil to a bowl of boiling water for an extra fragrance lift to free your mind from the mundane world. If you have identified a soul fragrance, it may prove an evocative trigger, either as the main or the background aroma.

Some people hate the idea of even visualising floating above their bodies. Using this technique, however, you do not need to travel upwards, as you will be entering your alternative reality through a door.

Do this exercise after dusk. You may decide in advance on a place you would like to visit (whether actual or mythical) or you can allow the experience to unfold spontaneously.

What you need: A scented candle; incense (optional); essential oil and a bowl of boiling water (optional).

✢ Go to your indoor fragrant place and light the scented candle. Light the incense and drop the essential oil into the bowl of water if you are using either of these.

✢ Sit or lie in a comfortable position and begin to breathe gently and regularly. With each in-breath picture the light from the candle enclosing you in coloured perfumed light.

✢ Imagine the candle flame becoming larger and more brilliant and see a doorway emerge. Begin to breathe yourself into the doorway of light.

✢ Let the door swing open. At first you may wish just to look through it.

✢ If and when you are ready, move forwards through the doorway, counting slowly from one to ten as you take ten steps forward into the astral world.

✢ What you find there is limited only by the extent of your imagination and the collective pool of unconscious human knowledge. There may be mountains, seas, other galactic systems, Atlantis or some realm of light where angels live. There may be holes in the ground leading to stairways to subterranean realms with talking animals, fairies, witches or wise magicians. You can float, fly, dive, swim, walk through walls and cross the earth in seconds, for this is a world not ruled by time or space. Here, dragons and alien star systems can be safely encountered because your mind is always in control of your experiences.

✢ Either allow the experience to end naturally or when you are ready to return count backwards from ten to one and walk back to the doorway. Go through it, this time exhaling the light as you breathe until you are conscious of sitting facing the candle once more. You may feel you have been away for days but in fact only a few minutes will have elapsed.

✢ When you are ready, scribble down images or words to remind you of your experience before it fades. When you study these later, you may find they offer help in making current decisions or clues to present opportunities.

✢ If you want to return to the same astral place on another occasion, simply visualise it as you inhale the fragrance.

Past-life recall

We cannot know for sure whether past lives are a reality, although the evidence, especially from young children, indicates that they may be. One theory suggests that so-called past-life experiences actually result from tapping into the life of an ancestor, perhaps one whose personality or life path was similar to our own. Another theory suggests that since all human life originated in East Africa, we are able to use a common gene to access remote relatives in other lands and times. On the other hand, psychologists would say that we use the symbolism of the past as a way of acknowledging aspects of our present world that our conscious mind is unable or unwilling to address, and that this can be very valuable therapeutically.

Past-life recall is perhaps the single most effective use of fragrance in psychic work. You will get the best results with timeless natural fragrances such as fields of lavender, rose gardens and pine forests. The aroma of a country garden, or an old house, or even a cathedral rich with frankincense can lead you back to scenes from the past – be they from a previous life or simply symbolically relevant to things going on in your current life.

A simple way to evoke past lives is to inhale fragrance from a glass dropper or bottle – as I did in the Cairo perfume maker's. Try doing this in your indoor fragrant place, prolonging the experience by lighting a scented candle and incense with an appropriate aroma.

Suitable fragrances for past-life work include cedarwood, copal, cypress, frankincense, hibiscus, hyacinth, jasmine, lavender, lilac, lotus, sweet marjoram, mimosa, myrrh, papyrus flower, rose, sage, thyme and sandalwood.

Exploring past lives

What you need: One of the past-life fragrances listed above and/or your soul fragrance; a scented candle (preferably beeswax, rose or lavender); a few grains of dried lavender or thyme.

✢ Go to your indoor fragrant place. Light the scented candle. If you are using your soul fragrance as an incense or oil, light that too.

✢ Inhale the past-life fragrance and your soul fragrance if you are using it in perfume form.

✢ Sprinkle the dried lavender or thyme in the candle flame, counting down from your present age in regular steps until you reach your conception, for example:

I am 30 years old, I am 25 years old ...

(When they reach conception, some people spontaneously experience glimpses of a place where tiny golden children play, a kind of preconception world of potential souls.)

✢ Right in the centre of the candlelight, picture a flight of steps leading to a garden. As in the astral travel exercise (see pages 99–100), breathe yourself into the light using the fragrance.

✣ Counting from one at the top to ten at the bottom, walk down the steps to reach the garden. There is a gate there. Walk through it or, if you prefer, remain at the gate looking outwards.

✣ Now look at the scene around you and see if you can identify the past world. You may see a figure with whom you feel close kinship and who shares your name. What you see is just a picture filtered through your imagination so nothing can hurt you. You will never witness your own death – even a symbolic one – and you can at any time end the experience by counting down from ten to one. You can enter any building or go anywhere you wish, for no one can see you and the normal physical restrictions do not apply. You can walk through walls or fly.

✣ Watch the person you feel closest to emotionally as they go about their work or interact with their family. As you observe their life, you may begin to understand your own fears or feelings, or see that you need to take an opportunity about which you have been undecided.

✣ When you are ready or if the figures appear to fade, walk back to the gate, return to the garden and count yourself up the steps of light from ten to one.

✣ Looking once more at the candle flame, count upwards in stages from nought until you reach your present age.

✣ While the experience is fresh in your mind, scribble down some notes. If you wish to return to the scene on another occasion, you can read them before beginning the session.

An outdoor past-life exploration

✣ As the light is fading, sit in your outdoor fragrant place or a park, garden or historical or religious building where the scents are particularly rich. Follow the instructions for the past-life exploration above, but instead of burning herbs in a candle, close your eyes and imagine flower petals floating down upon you. As above, visualise steps of light down which you walk into the past world.

✣ Return by counting yourself back up the steps.

Meditation page 102

...vood for past-life recall.

...)d of burning fragrant wood to evoke visions of ...:ribed by the twentieth-century occultist Dion ...vel *Sea Priestess*. She called this the Fire of ...:ter the Archangel who in Hebrew mythology ...ful of soil, from which God created Adam (and ...f the myth Lilith, Adam's first wife). The fire ...r wood, cedar and sandalwood. This fire, says ...isions of past worlds.

...ook, the Fire of Azrael is made in a hearth. If ...earth, however, you can make a bonfire, using ...and adding dried juniper berries, crumbled sandalwood incense and dried cedar leaves, or adding a few drops of sandalwood and cedarwood essential oil to the wood before lighting. Good places for a bonfire are on a beach, in a dug-out pit of stones and earth or in the garden. Alternatively, make a fire in a flameproof cauldron or barbecue dish. If none of these methods is possible, light a huge purple candle (lavender-scented if possible) in a bucket of sand, surrounded by incense sticks in cedar, juniper and sandalwood – or crumble the herbs in the flame.

My own favourite wood-burners are Mexican chimineas, free-standing stone chimneys. These are sold in garden centres and are ideal for fragrance-burning work, as well as for keeping you warm in the garden and for cooking kebabs or potatoes in the embers.

What you need: The makings of your fire (see above).

✣ Make your fire. Wait until it burns low and then, through half-closed eyes, look at the embers and flames (or the candle flame if you are using the candle method).

✣ Images of past worlds may appear in your mind's eye, or you may see scenes within the fire itself.

✣ Once you have finished working with a particular scene, you can poke the fire to create a new formation.

✣ When you have finished working, put out the fire thoroughly. Spend some time writing down what you saw, together with your impressions and feelings.

CHAPTER 8

Fragrance, Prayer and Angelic Communication

In ancient religions, fragrance – especially in the form of incense – carried the prayers of the faithful to the heavens. It was believed that fragrances were a gift of the gods and mortals might become more perfect by absorbing them.

Incense has been used in religious ceremonies throughout history and in cultures all over the world. The first known use of incense was in the religious ceremonies of the Assyrians and Babylonians. In the Old Testament, God commands Moses to build an altar of incense on which only the sweetest spices and gums are to be burned. The Mayans and the Aztecs burned copal incense on the flat platform tops of their step pyramids when they made sacrifices to the gods. In mediaeval times the correct use of incense was central to ceremonial magic, each incense having a magical and astrological meaning. In the Roman Catholic as well as Eastern and High Anglican churches incense still forms an important part of services. Although it has now entered homes as background ambience, incense nevertheless remains the most magical and mystical of all fragrance forms.

Fragrances and personal prayer

As children we may have prayed at night or in school assembly, but adults can feel self-conscious about praying. Nevertheless, in times of crisis, many of us instinctively turn to prayer. After September 11th, many Americans who had never thought of themselves as religious found themselves calling on the God or the Goddess for help.

Whether you belong to a traditional religion or whether you simply see divinity as present in all of creation, prayer can be a good way of connecting with higher powers. These powers may be regarded as external and separate from ourselves – a creator God or Goddess, an angelic form, a deva (or higher essence of nature) – or as abstractions – benevolent light, positive energy or the universal life force. They can also be regarded as our own inner spark of divinity that makes us a small part of that creator spirit ourselves, or as our own evolved spirit or soul, the part that may survive death.

While meditation leads us inwards to our spiritual core, prayer directs our spiritual energy outwards, externalising our feelings and expressing a desire for connection with a source of power wiser than ourselves that will hear our requests, worries and dreams and give a response – if only that we must wait or that what we seek may not be what we need. Sometimes when we externalise our feelings, fears, hopes and dreams in this way, the answer comes to us quite spontaneously, whether from God, the Goddess, an angel or our own wise spiritual self. Prayer can also be a way of voicing concerns about poverty, war, famine, cruelty to children and animals, pollution and global warming – things that seem to need more than merely human effort to get them back on track.

Prayer does not need to be formal. It can be like a heart-to-heart with a wise older person who can accept us as we are. Nor does it have to involve spoken words. It can be a song, a chant or music. Prayer can also be silent instinctive communication with the cosmos, or thanks for life and health and enough resources. It may be manifest as offerings left in a beautiful place, perhaps with written requests for healing for other people, help for endangered or ill-treated animals, or peace and plenty for war- and famine-torn places. These petitions may be tied to trees with ribbons. Prayer can also take the form of reading sacred literature or absorbing the atmosphere in a cathedral, Graeco-Roman temple, Hindu shrine, mosque, synagogue or other place in which people have held religious ceremonies for centuries. Alternatively, it may take place in a grove of trees, an old stone circle or a sacred place beneath the stars.

Through all of these prayer places and techniques, fragrance forms a thread, be it clouds of frankincense billowing on a high altar or the scented breeze of a pine grove in a pagan celebration. For aroma uplifts the spirit and carries the prayer energies upwards to the heavens and around the earth in the form of positive thoughts.

If you do not find any form of prayer appropriate in your life, you can use sacred incense burning as a focus for spontaneous connection with cosmic energies, drawing strength from the powers of both the natural world and the skies and perhaps coming to understand more of the sacred spark that I believe we all carry within us.

Incense-burning for prayer

Prayer with incense is most potent at sunrise or sunset, when the incense smoke rises against the scarlet of the sky.

For most outdoor prayer and personal ritual work incense sticks are preferable, being easy and safe to use – especially if you work on soil or sand, away from overhanging trees or dry grass. However, in a sheltered outdoor place or indoors, more traditional incense-burning, using a censer and non-combustible incense (i.e. not the stick form) on hot charcoal, can be a very valuable spiritual tool. This more formal method makes the act of incense-burning itself a sacred ceremony.

If you make incense prayer or contemplation sessions a regular part of your life, you will quickly find yourself becoming calmer, less subject to mood swings and more confident in your decisions and actions.

Traditional (non-combustible) incense

Some practitioners make their own incense. This can be very empowering, as you can endow the incense with blessings as you prepare it; however, it takes a considerable amount of time and is very messy. If you would like to have a go, Scott Cunningham's *Complete Book of Incense, Oils and Brews* (see page 182) is excellent and describes the process step by step.

A number of dried herbs, flower petals and barks will burn on a heated charcoal block and release fragrant smoke without any preparation. These include small dried flowers such as chamomile, hibiscus and lavender heads; dried leaves such as bay, sage, rosemary and thyme (you can use the culinary herbs); wood chips such as cinnamon or sandalwood; pine needles; and juniper berries. Make sure they are very dry and chopped finely. Test a few grains initially, as sometimes the burnt aroma is different from the scent of the plant.

If you are new to using traditional incense, however, you are best advised to buy prepared granules or powder. Commercial incense powders and pastes are mixed with resins such as dragon's blood and gum Arabic (from the acacia tree) and are almost guaranteed to burn well and release fragrant smoke for a much longer period than the home-made and completely natural varieties. Keep a supply of your favourite traditional incenses in dark glass jars to protect them from light. You can use up to three fragrances together at one time, but burn a small quantity to see if they mix before you use them in ritual.

Traditional incense is burnt on charcoal. The easiest type to work with comes in individual discs about the size of a large coin. These discs have an indentation in the centre, on which you scatter your incense when the charcoal is hot. You can buy charcoal discs from New Age stores, shops that deal in Indian goods and even some hardware stores. You also can buy larger charcoal mini-briquettes, but for most home rituals you will not need anything of this size.

To burn traditional incense you also need a censer to hold the burning charcoal. This is a lidded metal dish with holes for the smoke to come out – the kind of thing used in high church services, temple ceremonies and formal magic. Censers can be bought from New Age stores, church shops and shops that deal in Indian goods. A small one will be quite adequate. If you buy a censer with a chain, you can harmonise the fragrant smoke clouds with your words by swinging it. If you do not have a censer, use a flat heatproof dish with a lip (for carrying) and place a layer of sand or earth in the bottom of it.

Traditional prayer incenses include allspice, benzoin, cinnamon, cedar, cloves, copal, frankincense, gum Arabic (acacia), hibiscus, juniper, myrrh, pine, sage, sandalwood and thyme.

Burning traditional incense for prayer and ritual

What you need: Traditional incense(s) of your choice, charcoal, barbecue tongs, long cook's matches or a taper, a metal tray (if you are working indoors), a censer or heatproof dish, a small dish (to contain your incense prior to burning).

✢ Place the censer on the metal tray if you are working indoors. If you are working outdoors, place the censer on a safe stable surface such as earth or concrete.

✢ Pick up your charcoal in the barbecue tongs and hold it over the censer or dish as you light one edge with the cook's matches or taper (safer and easier than using ordinary matches). Keep the charcoal in contact with the match or taper until it starts to spark.

✢ Place the charcoal in the censer. It is sometimes hard initially to tell if charcoal is alight; however, if you blow or fan gently, you should see a glow. Do not touch the disk, as it will be very hot even if it has gone out. Once the charcoal is lit, you need to wait about five to ten minutes for it to turn greyish-white (white-hot) before you can burn your incense. (If you buy fast-lighting charcoal, this process will be quicker.)

✢ While you are waiting, set a small quantity of your chosen incense(s) on the dish and ask for blessings or powers to enter it as appropriate to your work. You can also use this time for quiet contemplation, to formulate your thoughts or to read a passage from a sacred work. You could pick a passage from the Bible or the I Ching or even a book of poetry at random; your 'chance' selection will invariably shed light on whatever it is you are working or praying for. (This art is called bibliomancy.)

✢ When the charcoal is white-hot, drop just a few herbs or granules in the centre of the disc, certainly no more than half a teaspoonful, adding them a bit at a time. (The old-fashioned tiny sugar spoons are ideal for this if you can get hold of one.) As the smoke rises from the first grains either say a formal prayer, chant from your favourite tradition or speak in your own words from your heart as though to a wise kind father or mother. If speaking does not seem appropriate, remain silent – words may come into your mind.

✢ Now make your requests or blessings. If you are using a censer, swing it after each one. You can add more incense, mixing the fragrances according to your need.

✢ When you have finished your work, wait for the incense to die down. You may be rewarded with some kind of sign, such as a sudden burst of sunshine, an increase in fragrance even though the heat of the charcoal is diminishing or a sense of being protected.

Praying with smudge sticks

This form of prayer takes place outdoors.

What you need: A sage smudge stick

✢ Light your smudge stick as described on page 60.

✢ Smudge each of the four directions in turn, as you do so using your own words to praise the four Grandfathers of the North, East, South and West.

✢ Smudge the earth, as you do so praising Mother Earth. Now raise the smudge stick to the skies, as you do so praising Father Sky. You can now ask for a blessing.

✢ When you have finished praying, put out your smudge stick safely.

Angels and fragrance

It has been hypothesised by angelologists (those who study angelic lore through the ages) that there are millions of angels. Therefore even the weightiest angel encyclopaedia identifies only a relatively small number of angels – mainly archangels, warrior angels, fallen angels and those associated with ceremonial magic or the mystical literature of traditional religions. The majority of angels seen or sensed by ordinary people are not identifiable under any formal system.

Many of those who have experienced an angelic presence or regularly communicate with a guardian angel speak of an accompanying fragrance that is not quite earthly and has a wonderful purity. For example Chloe, an American woman I met while giving a workshop in Sweden, talks to an angel whose presence is preceded by a rose aroma. She describes this as smelling like the most perfect rose garden in the world. Having talked to a number of people such as Chloe who have encountered angels and having researched angel lore, I have come to the conclusion that, like humans, many guardian angels have an identifiable signature fragrance that enables us to contact them in times of need via a pathway of fragrance, for example through burning prayer incense.

The different angelic signature fragrances seem to reflect the qualities offered to humans by particular angels or angelic energies and are therefore an effective means by which we can absorb these qualities into our own lives, even if we do not believe literally in angels. In fact, some people are of the opinion that angels are not really separate objective beings but rather energy vibrations that our minds interpret in a certain way within the limitations of human understanding.

The fragrances that have been described as accompanying angels (or angelic energies) are predominantly floral and have been identified variously as apple blossom, carnation, geranium, hibiscus, honeysuckle, hyacinth, jasmine, lavender, lilac, lilies, linden blossom, lotus, mimosa, orange blossom (neroli), rose and violet. However, you may encounter other fragrances in your angelic explorations and can work with these just as easily.

Fragrance angels

Fragrance angels are the angelic energies attached to particular fragrances. There are many ways in which you can work with them, for example by burning a particular fragrance as a scented candle, incense or oil. You can also smell the fragrance as cologne or add it to a bath and visualise the angel's presence.

You may find that different fragrance angels naturally move close at different times in your life. You may, for instance, suddenly start smelling a wonderful violet fragrance at a time when you are feeling a strong need for secrecy, perhaps connected with revealing your love for someone. On the other hand, you could take the initiative and call on the Violet Angel (or her energies) by burning violet oil to help you cope if, say, you were suddenly entrusted with information you must not reveal.

Try spending time working with some of the angelic energies listed below. The physical characteristics I give have been described for me by people who have approached angels through fragrances. Use them to get you started, but don't feel that you have to stick with them if your angel turns out to look different.

The Apple Blossom Angel

✢ This angel is the guardian of health, healing and fertility, and is concerned with all who have health problems or care for sick or disabled relatives. She will also help anyone trying for a baby or who is pregnant or a new parent.

✢ She offers hope and counsels patience, encouraging us to get back in touch with our own life cycle and with the changing seasons of nature.

✢ Visualise her in pale pink-and-white clouds or mists, or surrounded by falling blossoms. She is delicate and pale, and sometimes accompanied by tiny angels.

✢ Call on her with her fragrance if you need fertility of any kind in your life or are exhausted.

The Carnation Angel

✢ The Carnation angel is the guardian of the family and of family traditions. She attaches herself especially to older people, but she will also help with matters of justice and injustice, whether legal or private disputes, from playground bullying to the threat of losing your home.

✢ She is slow to speak and judge, and will always counsel avoiding rash words or hasty actions.

✢ Visualise her as a mature woman with a serious expression, wearing white, with scarlet-tipped wings.

✢ Call on her with her fragrance if you need to take on officialdom or if your confidence is being eroded by a critical employer or controlling lover.

The Geranium Angel

✢ The Geranium angel is associated with sleep and dreams. She moves close to those who live frantic lives and suffer the stress of juggling the demands of work and home. She also helps anyone struggling against phobias or who is trying to quit compensatory habits such as comfort eating or smoking.

✢ She offers a sanctuary from the world and counsels listening to your body and to your inner voice in order to discover your own natural rhythms.

✣ Picture her appearing through swirls of pink, mauve and misty blue, enveloping protectively in her soft blue cloak all who are worried or overwhelmed.

✣ Call on her with her fragrance if you are suffering from insomnia or bad dreams, or are trying to do too much out of necessity and feel out of tune with the world.

The Hibiscus Angel

✣ She is the angel of warm sun-drenched lands. She attaches herself to creative people – those in the media and all those who love singing, dancing, acting or writing – as well as those who desperately want to develop their artistic talents but lack confidence in them. She also helps people who have become depressed or feel that life is passing them by.

✣ She offers inspiration and counsels developing buried potential and reviving lost dreams.

✣ Visualise this wonderfully exotic angel with a skin burnished by the sun, dressed in bright pink, red, orange and yellow, and constantly moving.

✣ Call on her with her fragrance if you want to change the emphasis in your life to make it more personally fulfilling or to bring laughter and spontaneity into your world once more.

The Honeysuckle Angel

✣ She is determined and tenacious. She attaches herself to people who are rebuilding their lives and who need to persevere in order to progress. She also blesses those who support difficult relatives and those involved in relationships that are going through a bad patch. She knows that patience will win through.

✣ She offers light at the end of the tunnel and counsels valuing and caring for ourselves as well as others.

✣ Visualise her as a deceptively delicate angel with pink, yellow and purple-edged wings. Green tendrils grow and twine around her.

✣ Call on her with her fragrance when you are worried about an examination or keeping your job in uncertain times, or if you need to exercise tough love with awkward people you care for.

The Hyacinth Angel

✢ A messenger of spring, she attaches herself mainly to children and younger people who are setting out on the road to independence, but also people who live alone, whether from choice or necessity. She helps anyone who is beginning a new venture (for example self-employment), who works alone or who follows a private dream.

✢ She offers the knowledge that being alone is not the same as loneliness and counsels a new beginning or fresh perspective to shift stagnation and inertia.

✢ Visualise her in a pink-and-purple robe, covered with spring flowers of all kinds and with a profusion of flowers in her hands.

✢ Call on her with her fragrance if you need to find the spring, for new beginnings at any time in your life and for self-love.

The Jasmine Angel

✢ As a lunar angel, she is mistress of mystery and imagination. She attaches herself to women at transitions in their lives and to all who seek to explore their own spirituality and to develop their psychic gifts.

✢ She offers the knowledge that life ebbs and flows and does not run in straight lines, and counsels trusting your intuition rather than being led by what others say you should do or feel.

✢ Visualise her bathed in silver moonlight, with silver wings and a halo of the full moon surmounted by the crescent.

✢ Call on her with her fragrance when you doubt yourself or feel ready to move into the next phase of your life.

The Lavender Angel

✢ The gentlest of the angels, she protects all who are soft-natured and quietly spoken, and who sometimes get overlooked or overridden. She also cares for animal-lovers and those who work to improve the environment.

✢ She offers the knowledge that kind words and deeds will always defeat spite and anger, and counsels not allowing anyone to change your loving approach to life.

✣ Visualise her knee-deep in fields of lavender, her wings stained with purple flowers that she gathers in her arms.

✣ Call on her with her fragrance to develop your own healing powers and to shield you from cruelty or malice.

The Lilac Angel

✣ The angel of the home and domestic happiness, she is close to the Carnation angel. She attaches herself to all homemakers and those who make others feel welcome, whether by creating a friendly corner in the office or sparing the time to listen.

✣ She offers the knowledge that the home, even if we live there alone, is the secure base from which we can explore the world. She counsels valuing those who form our family unit in the world, whether related to us or not.

✣ Visualise her as amply proportioned and welcoming, more like a countrywoman than a typical angel.

✣ Call upon her with her fragrance for help with home moves, renovations and any domestic matter, and when you feel you need to touch home base when far away from home.

The Lily Angel

✣ She has an aura of quiet strength about her and brings the courage to resist emotional pressure and to remain harmonious within. She attaches herself to those living in turbulent times or experiencing emotionally charged relationships. She also helps to counter personal mood swings and unhappiness about what cannot be changed.

✣ She offers the knowledge that all will be well if you find your own inner harmony and counsels that you listen to what your heart tells you at quiet moments rather than guilt feelings and others' appeals to your sentiments.

✣ Visualise her wearing an unadorned white robe and looking like a nun except for her long, flowing almost-white hair.

✣ Call on her with her fragrance when you feel you are being manipulated emotionally or you are worrying too much about hurting the feelings of others and so hurting yourself.

The Linden Blossom Angel

✥ An angel of the dawn, whose yellow-and-white blossoms grow on the lime tree, she expands the horizons of possibility, attaching herself to all who travel or who seek to widen their personal or intellectual horizons. She blesses those who are open-minded and eager to understand different lifestyles.

✥ She offers the knowledge that life is all about change and movement, and counsels that you seek new people and places if you cannot find what you need in your present life.

✥ Visualise her as almost boyish with an eager expression, wearing a yellow-and-white tunic and holding in her hand a map that she may one day show you.

✥ Call on her with her fragrance if you know there is more to life and you need the courage to explore and make innovations.

The Lotus Angel

✥ An angel of the sun at dawn and at sunset, she seeks the highest good, attaching herself to crusaders and idealists. She also blesses those who – perhaps unwillingly – take on leadership or responsibilities on behalf of others who cannot speak effectively for themselves.

✥ She offers a new opportunity with each sunrise and the washing away of what is not worth conserving with each dusk. She counsels avoiding regrets about yesterday or worries about tomorrow.

✥ Visualise her like a classical goddess, tall and statuesque, with a golden bow and quiver of arrows.

✥ Call on her with her fragrance when you need to speak out or act boldly in spite of opposition from the status quo.

The Mimosa Angel

✥ She is the wisest of the fragrance angels. She attaches herself to those who seek personal fulfilment rather than success and wealth, and who are searching for meaning in their lives.

✥ She offers a future that is ours to make and counsels against allowing ourselves to follow paths shaped by other people's dreams or standards of attainment.

✣ Visualise her as serene and still, with the clusters of creamy white star-like mimosa blossoms on her brow for which she is called the Star Angel.

✣ Call on her with her fragrance to recall lost dreams and buried identity and to follow your own destiny.

The Orange Blossom Angel

✣ The Orange Blossom angel is also serene but her serenity comes through knowledge of human frailty and yet faith in the ultimate goodness of humanity. She attaches herself to all who are entering into a permanent relationship, whether for the first, second or third time, or in a love of late maturity. She blesses all faithful lovers as well as partners who have survived tests in their relationship and come through stronger.

✣ She offers the undying hope that we will find true love and counsels against valuing excitement over loyalty.

✣ Visualise her wearing an orange-blossom crown and carrying a basket of oranges, scattering a shower of flowers as she walks.

✣ Call on her with her fragrance when you are making a commitment to another person or seeking to save a relationship that is going through a bad patch.

The Rose Angel

✣ She is the angel of love and healing. She attaches herself to those who have open loving hearts and offer friendship without counting the cost. She also helps anyone in pain – emotional or physical.

✣ She offers us the knowledge that we can heal our own past hurt best by caring for others, and counsels mending old quarrels and dissolving any coldness that has grow up with those we love, even if we were not at fault.

✣ Visualise her surrounded by roses of every colour and kind, from tiny rosebuds to full-blown flowers.

✣ Call on her with her fragrance if you have suffered any kind of abuse, if you are young and in love or in love for the first time, or if you are entering into a new friendship or romance after sorrow or betrayal.

The Violet Angel

✢ She is the guardian of hidden matters – particularly secrets relating to unrequited love and relationships in their earliest stages. She attaches herself to all who must remain silent for the time being and also to those who work in the background or as support staff in any organisation or enterprise.

✢ She offers the knowledge that now is the time of waiting and counsels that gaining the trust of others through our discretion is a great privilege.

✢ Visualise her dimly seen in a violet haze, only occasionally lifting her veil and speaking very softly.

✢ Call on her using her fragrance if you must hide your true feelings for the sake of others or must wait for your talents to be recognised.

An aromatic bath to identify your fragrance angel

This fragrant milk bath is an effective way of identifying the angel with whom you feel most in tune, as well as of experiencing or recreating otherworldly aromas. Try it if you have not yet experienced an angelic presence but would like to do so.

Carry out this ritual on different nights with different angelic fragrances. You may sense or see angels around you quite vividly with several of the fragrances, but one in particular will evoke an angel with whom you feel a sense of kinship. You may perceive her in some indefinable way or you may catch a glimpse of her.

Once you have identified the fragrance of your special angel, repeat the bathing experience using this fragrance on two or three subsequent occasions and you will get clearer and more detailed impressions of your personal guardian and perhaps hear her voice in your mind. A more specific name may come into your mind associated with your special angel, which you can check in an angelology book if you wish – bear in mind, however, that, as I said, catalogued angels represent only a small proportion of those encountered through the ages.

What you need: 250 ml/8 fl oz/1 cup fresh full-fat or reconstituted powdered milk containing vegetable fat, up to 10 drops of one of the angelic fragrances as essential oil (with fragrances for which there is no essential oil – for example honeysuckle, lilac and lily – use petals to make a herbal infusion or bath sachet [see pages 77–81], or buy a natural floral bath product in the fragrance), sacred choral music (for example Gregorian or Buddhist chants), a white unscented pillar candle or tall beeswax candle, an incense stick in your chosen angelic fragrance.

✦ Fill a bath with warm water and add the milk, swirling it in the water. Add the essential oil – it will be dissolved by the milk.

✦ Turn on the music and light the incense and pillar candle. Place the candle where you will be able to see it easily from the bath.

✦ Get in the bath, inhale the perfume and through half-closed eyes allow an angelic form to build up around the candle or in your mind's eye. You may create an outline if you wish, or you may prefer the experience to be entirely spontaneous. Don't worry if the angel you see differs from the ones described above, as we all see the angelic energies in our own unique way. Do not speak unless the angelic form speaks to you, but as the figure fades, thank the angelic presence for appearing and ask for angelic protection.

✦ After your bath, draw the angel you saw and write down any characteristics you noticed.

Contacting your personal angel

Once you have clearly identified your personal angel by her fragrance, you can contact her when you are sitting quietly in the evening in your indoor or outdoor fragrant place or in your bedroom before sleep. Have flowers, blossoms, cologne or pot pourri made from the angelic fragrance to use as a focus. Alternatively, you can paint your angel or craft her in clay – you do not need to be artistic as this will be your private representation and can be as abstract as you wish. As an alternative to the beeswax candle used in this ritual, you can burn the relevant angelic incense close to any type of candle or simply use the relevant scented candle.

If you need the strength of any of the other angels you can also use the following method and the relevant fragrance to ask that angel to help you.

What you need: A beeswax candle, 1–4 drops of the relevant angelic essential oil or fragrance oil.

✤ Light the candle and, when the wax is melted into a deep well, blow it out. Beeswax is potent for angelic work as bees are traditionally messengers, like angels, between the earth and the heavens.

✤ Drop the essential or fragrance oil into the wax, being careful not to get any oil on the wick. Relight the candle as the wax solidifies.

✤ Gaze into the flame and as you inhale the fragrance allow a picture of your angel to build up in your mind's eye or in the aura around the candle. If you find this difficult, let your eyes half close and picture the aura of the candle expanding to fill the darkness. Close your eyes, open them and then blink and smile. In the light you will see your angel smiling back, radiating an all-encompassing love and protection. If you don't see this, imagine it until your psyche kicks in.

✤ You need not do anything or say anything, but you can if you wish ask questions or enquire whether your angel has a special message for you. You may hear a soft but clear voice in your ear that is like your own inner voice but of a purer quality. Those who do not believe in angels consider this to be your higher self talking – which makes the experience no less valuable.

✤ When you sense the energies fading, thank your angel, blow out the candle and send the angelic light to all who need it, not forgetting yourself.

In the course of the next chapter we will be working with the seven ceremonial archangels (see pages 128–36).

CHAPTER 9
Fragrance, Astrology and Divination

The semi-divine first-century Egyptian sorcerer Hermes Trismesgistos, whose Emerald Tablet was said to contain the secrets of all magic, stated, 'As Above, so Below', thus establishing the connection between cosmic and earthly realms that is still the basic tenet of both magic and astrology today. Like others over the millennia, from Babylon to the ceremonial magicians of the early twentieth century, Hermes Trismesgistos was convinced that astrological forces might by earthly associations, such as specific fragrances, be used to increase human power and give access to knowledge beyond the reach of the conscious human mind.

Each of the seven planets and 12 zodiacal signs has a specific fragrance that represents its most positive qualities. These astrological strengths can be activated and absorbed by inhaling the aromas as living plants or perfumes, by burning them as incense or oils, or by adding them to the bath.

Sun sign fragrances

Most potent for an individual is his or her sun sign fragrance, which can be used to boost personal power instantly at any time. The period when the sun is actually in your particular sign is the most potent time of all for using your fragrance. In the following table, the fragrant associations of each sign are drawn from a number of different traditions. (Note that the actual dates of each sign vary by a day or two from year to year; for precise dates consult an ephemeris.)

♈ Aries, the ram (21 March–20 April)

Characteristics: Assertiveness, self-confidence, innovation, enterprise, ingenuity, independence, strong sense of identity

Herbs: Peppermint, thyme
Trees/woods: Pine
Flowers: Carnation, honeysuckle

♉ Taurus, the bull (21 April–21 May)

Characteristics: Persistence, patience, reliability, loyalty, practical abilities, stability, love of beauty
Herbs: Chamomile, vervain
Trees/woods: Apple
Flowers: Lilac, rose

♊ Gemini, the heavenly twins (22 May–21 June)

Characteristics: Excellent communication skills, adaptability, scientific/technological aptitude, intelligence, versatility
Herbs: Dill, lemongrass
Trees/woods: Almond
Flowers: Lavender, lily of the valley

♋ Cancer, the crab (22 June–22 July)

Characteristics: Sensitivity, kindness, imagination, homemaking and nurturing (especially of children), creation of emotional security, ability to keep secrets
Herbs: Lemon verbena, melissa (lemon balm)
Trees/woods: Eucalyptus
Flowers: Gardenia, jasmine

♌ Leo, the lion (23 July–23 August)

Characteristics: Power, courage, generosity, nobility, idealism, protection of the weak, ability to perform in public
Herbs: Frankincense, orange
Trees/woods: Bay
Flowers: Marigold, sunflower

♍ Virgo, the maiden (24 August–22 September)

Characteristics: Striving for perfection, organisational skills, methodical attention to detail, efficiency, healing powers, perseverance, ability to carry through routine tasks, reliability
Herbs: Fennel, patchouli
Trees/woods: Cypress
Flowers: Lavender, lily

♎ Libra, the scales (23 September–23 October)

Characteristics: Harmony, ability to see both sides of a question and incorporate different viewpoints, diplomacy, peace-making skills, strong sense of justice, charisma
Herbs: Marjoram, vanilla
Trees/woods: Peach
Flowers: Hydrangea, ylang ylang

♏ Scorpio, the scorpion (24 October–22 November)

Characteristics: Intensity, psychic awareness, ability to transform self, power to start over again or revive an unpromising or stagnant situation
Herbs: Basil, ginger
Trees/woods: Sandalwood
Flowers: Mimosa, geranium

♐ Sagittarius, the archer (23 November–21 December)

Characteristics: Expansiveness, love of travel and exploration, clear vision, seeking after truth, wide perspectives, flexibility, open-mindedness, optimism, boundless enthusiasm, creativity
Herbs: Anise, sage
Trees/woods: Lime
Flowers: Hibiscus, orange blossom (neroli)

♑ Capricorn, the goat (22 December–20 January)

Characteristics: Wise caution, persistence no matter what the opposition, respect for tradition, tried and tested methods, ambition, self-discipline, prudence in financial affairs
Herbs: Myrrh, vetivert
Trees/woods: Rosewood
Flowers: Magnolia, hyacinth

♒ Aquarius, the water carrier (21 January–18 February)

Characteristics: Idealism, independence, humanitarianism, inventiveness, detachment from swings of emotion and prejudices, unique perspective on the world
Herbs: Benzoin, rosemary
Trees/woods: Flowering cherry
Flowers: Acacia, orchid

⊁ Pisces, the fish (19 February–20 March)

Characteristics: Evolved intuitive powers, sympathy, empathy, weaving of myths, awareness of hidden factors, ability to merge with surroundings
Herbs: Sweetgrass, musk (artificial)
Trees/woods: Lemon
Flowers: Sweet pea, lotus

There are a number of ways to use your birth fragrance:

✛ Add culinary herbs such as bay, sage and thyme to meals.

✛ Holding a flower or aromatic herb, breathe in the fragrance , visualising it as an appropriately coloured light.

✛ Carry empowered or enchanted dried herbs or flowers (see pages 27–32) in a small purse or add them to your morning bath on an important day.

✛ If you are feeling under pressure at work, a small vase or pot of your birth flowers or a dish of dried herbs on your desk will protect you from stress and bring out your natural strengths and coping abilities.

✛ Keep a birth sign fragrance spray in your bag or desk drawer for an instant burst of power before a difficult phone call or meeting.

✛ Take a small room-spray bottle (see page 51) of your birth sign fragrance to work to counter the effects of air conditioning or central heating in your personal workspace.

Borrowing zodiacal power

As well as using your own sun sign fragrance, you can also borrow those of other signs, using them to import mental and emotional strengths when you need them. For example, if you are a placid Taurus, you might need to borrow the courage of Aries to start at a new workplace where you have been promoted over an existing member of staff. In this case, a drink of peppermint tea or a dish of thyme next to your computer will keep your Aries determination going all day and create a protective screen against those who might be unhelpful. If you are a sensitive Cancerian who hates talking in public and you have to give a presentation, you could try borrowing some of Gemini's sociability by eating almonds. Add the showmanship of Leo by adding a few bay leaves to a casserole the night before and you will win a standing ovation.

Planetary fragrances

The planets also have their special fragrances. Planetary aromas tend to be slower-acting but accumulate concentrated power. They can be used if you have a long-term goal or need to build up your physical, mental or emotional power, perhaps after a setback or if you are working towards an examination and need to focus your concentration and improve your memory.

The planet that rules your sun sign will always be the one whose fragrance will help to keep you on track or put you back there if your confidence has taken a knock, but you can also adopt a planetary aroma whose qualities you feel would help to develop you spiritually or prepare you emotionally for a life change.

Where, as sometimes happens, a herb or flower is both a birth sign and a planetary fragrance it can be used both for long- and short-term power. Lemongrass, for example, belongs to both the sun sign Gemini and its ruling planet Mercury. For more long-term intellectual powers you could use it to make pot pourri, planting the herb in your outdoor fragrant place, as these natural forms of the life force permeate your body gradually with an effect that is long-lasting. For a quick burst of mercurial intellectual ability, you could pick some of your lemongrass the night before an examination and take it with you as a talisman.

Make planetary fragrances part of your fragrance shelf store. You can add them in small quantities to your nightly baths or burn them regularly in the home as oils to gradually empower your system and your life.

In accordance with traditional magical practice, in the list below I have given only the five ancient planets that can be seen without a telescope, along with the sun and the moon (not strictly speaking planets but regarded as such in magic). Each of these planets is a ruler or co-ruler of one of the sun signs. The more distant planets Uranus, Neptune and Pluto are very slow-moving and though they have been assigned the rulership of sun signs in modern astrology, they do not work so well in fragrance magic or indeed any spiritual work.

The sun ☉

✦ The sun rules Leo.

✦ Use the sun as a focus for personal fulfilment, ambition, power and success, for asserting or strengthening your identity, for innovation of all kinds and for new beginnings in your life. It is potent for energy, joy, good health, self-confidence and for bringing or restoring prosperity when fortunes are low. It will also break a run of bad luck.

✦ The sun's fragrances include acacia, angelica, bay, benzoin, carnation, chamomile, copal, frankincense, juniper, lime, lotus, marigold, orange, rosemary (also ruled by Mercury), saffron, St John's wort and tangerine.

The moon ☽

✦ The moon rules Cancer.

✦ Use the moon as focus for matters concerning the home and family, mothers, children, animals, fertility and all the ebbs and flows of the human body, mind and psyche. It can also be used for protection of all kinds, as well as for psychic development, clairvoyance and meaningful dreams. Work with the moon if you are creating a beautiful garden for healing or if you need to keep a secret.

✦ The moon's fragrances include coconut, eucalyptus, gardenia, jasmine, lemon, melissa (lemon balm), lotus (also ruled by the sun), myrrh, poppy and tea tree.

Mercury ☿

✦ Mercury rules Gemini and Virgo.

✦ Use Mercury as a focus for long term money-making ventures and reducing debts, for developing channels of clear communication or for getting a job in the media or in a technological or scientific field. Mercury is effective for improving memory and sharpening logic, for learning, examinations and tests, and for conventional methods of healing, especially surgery. Work with Mercury if someone is trying to damage your reputation or career by a prolonged whispering campaign.

✢ Mercury's fragrances include almond, dill, fennel, lavender, lemongrass, lily of the valley, parsley, rosemary and valerian.

Venus ♀

✢ Venus rules Taurus and Libra.

✢ Use Venus as a focus for attracting new love, for deepening existing love and for affection and fidelity in long-term relationships. Venus will also assist in increasing beauty, both personal and environmental; developing gifts and expertise in the arts, crafts and music; mending quarrels; slowly but surely increasing prosperity; and improving health. Like the moon, she can be invoked for fertility and for women's health matters, as well as for horticulture.

✢ Venus's fragrances include apple blossom, cherry blossom, echinacea, feverfew, geranium, hyacinth, lilac, lilies, magnolia, peach, rose, rosewood, strawberry, vanilla, vervain and ylang ylang.

Mars ♂

✢ Mars rules Aries and Scorpio.

✢ Use Mars energies for courage, instigating change and taking the initiative, working towards independence or self-employment, drawing the boundaries between self and others and healthy competition and assertiveness. Mars rules passion, the consummation of love and justifiable controlled anger in defence of the vulnerable.

✢ Mars's fragrances include allspice, basil, coriander (cilantro), cypress, dragon's blood, ginger, hibiscus, mint, passionflower, pine, tarragon and thyme.

Jupiter ♃

✢ Jupiter rules Sagittarius and Pisces.

✢ Use Jupiter as a focus for all forms of increase and expansion, whether improving fortune, career prospects or obtaining promotion. Use it also for joy through fulfilment of ambitions and for creating and preserving marriages and partnerships. It is also potent for leadership, maintaining integrity, resolving matters of justice and the law, and for travel or relocation plans.

✢ Jupiter's fragrances include anise, cedarwood, cloves, honeysuckle, linden blossom, meadowsweet, nutmeg, sage and sandalwood.

Saturn ♄

✢ Saturn rules Capricorn and Aquarius.

✢ Use Saturn as a focus for unfinished business, for endings that lead to beginnings, for all slow-moving matters, for accepting limitations and for overcoming obstacles that are long-standing or need careful handling. Saturn can help in relieving chronic pain, lifting depression or doubts and regaining self-control over bad habits or emotions. Saturn can also slow down the outward flow of money and encourage those who owe you money or favours to repay (even if this takes time).

✢ Saturn's fragrances include cypress, hyacinth, lemon verbena, mimosa, pansy, patchouli, sweet marjoram and vetivert.

Divining for an astrological fragrance

In most cases you will be sure of the direction in which you want to move and the things you want to achieve and can choose your astro-aroma accordingly. At other times, however, you may not be quite so sure where you are heading and what you need. You may sense a change in the air or feel restless. You may be aware of undercurrents at work or at home that are bubbling near the surface but feel unsure whether the time is ripe for confrontation, conciliation or keeping your counsel. When logic cannot determine the best course of action, it is possible to use divination to understand the potential paths that are open to you. After all, it is no good being fired up with your Mars ginger biscuits if outspokenness could cost you your job. You might have done better to wash your hair in a vanilla-based shampoo, which would have made you the voice of reason when the managing director descended from head office with a unknown agenda.

The following are a couple of methods you can use to divine for the most appropriate astrological fragrance. Neither of these methods is a random choice; they make use of psychokinesis, our innate psychic power. The unconscious mind guides the pendulum or our hand to choose the sun sign or planet whose fragrance will empower us or protect us from harm in the situation in question.

Divining for a fragrance with a pendulum

What you need: A pendulum, this book.

✢ Decide whether you are going to use sun sign or planetary fragrances.

✢ Move your pendulum slowly over the sun sign or planetary glyphs listed in this book on pages 120–3 and 125–7. Hold it 2–3 cm/1 in above the page. Let your mind go blank and allow the pendulum to pull down over the relevant glyph. You will probably also experience a tingling in your fingers over the correct choice – one that may not be at all what you expected but which will subsequently be justified.

Divining for a fragrance with crystals or stones

What you need: 19 coin-sized white stones or crystals with a flat surface, a fine-line permanent marker or a thin brush and acrylic paint, 2 drawstring bags.

✢ Draw or paint the 12 sun sign glyphs and seven planetary glyphs on the stones or crystals using the marker or brush and acrylic paint.

✢ Place the two sets of glyphs in separate drawstring bags.

✢ To divine for a sun sign or planetary fragrance, without looking, pick a stone from the appropriate bag.

The archangels and fragrance

The fragrance work we did with guardian angels in the previous chapter was within a very personal system. In angelology, guardian angels (our fragrance angels) are closest to individuals; archangels rank above angels and therefore have less personalised relationships with people. They are usually the main focus in magic because they represent archetypal or idealised qualities and have the power and authority to offer protection.

Angelology is a very complex – and sometimes confusing and contradictory – area of knowledge spanning thousands of years and many cultures. In formal religion angels are often defined as beings of light or spiritual energy and are found in Judaism, Christianity and Islam. Mediaeval angelology has linked the seven main archangels (whose names vary according to different traditions) with the seven planets. Each has a fragrance that can be used to call him close to us and enable us to connect with the wisdom of this higher being.

Archangels do not chat to us in the way that fragrance angels do, and archangel fragrance rituals therefore tend to be more formal. The communication is less about our earthly needs and more about the development of our spiritual strengths and altruistic qualities – though not necessarily in an abstract way. For example, you might ask kind Anael, the angel aligned with Venus, to soften your tongue and give you the patience of an angel when dealing with an elderly relative whose memory is failing.

The following is information about the seven Archangels. You can find out more from books (see page 181). You may also discover other archangels whose energies seem relevant to your life. If you cannot find out what their fragrances are, burn different aromas as you visualise the archangel. One or two scents will evoke the angelic presence strongly. Note these in your journal.

Archangel Michael

✢ Michael is archangel of the sun, of noon and of light. He is a warrior prince, resplendent in scarlet and gold. As commander of the heavenly hosts, he is usually pictured with a sword, driving Satan and his fallen angels out of the celestial realms or crushing a dragon beneath his winged feet. Angel of judgement, he also carries a scale to weigh the souls of the dead. Michael the initiator brings illumination and inspiration to spiritual life, offering glimpses of higher realms but always demanding the highest of standards and that we act rather than make vague plans. He is the guardian of all who are not prepared to compromise their ideals or integrity. He also works to revive barren land despoiled by industrialisation and to cleanse the air of pollution.

✛ His fragrances are frankincense and orange.

✛ Call on Michael for work to make the world a better place, for refusal to sacrifice personal principles for profit, for kickstarting your spiritual work if you have become unenthusiastic or unfocused, and for working towards your spiritual goals even if no one else can understand why you are bothering. Ask him also for illumination on questions about life that puzzle you or old problems with which you have struggled for years.

✛ Sunday is Michael's day, when his presence can most easily be sensed.

Archangel Gabriel

✛ Gabriel is archangel of the moon and of the evening and night, and is the most feminine of the archangels, wearing robes of silver and a crescent moon as a halo. He is the messenger archangel and as such is the easiest to connect with, either indoors or outdoors, on moonlit nights or in the darkness where fragrant jasmine blossoms. You may also see Gabriel in dreams if you burn his fragrances before you sleep. The integrator, he brings spirituality to the home and the workplace. He takes away grief and sorrow, and diminishes self-destructive tendencies, replacing them with the increasing awareness that the body and mind are the temple of our soul and so should be cherished. He protects also against the effects of storm, whirlwind and floods; guards endangered water creatures; and cleanses polluted seas, lakes and rivers.

✛ Gabriel's fragrances are myrrh and jasmine.

✛ Call on Gabriel for hope and a new sense of purpose, for the development of compassion for others and for acceptance of your own weaknesses. Ask him for help in tuning into your personal ebbs and flows of spiritual energy and in translating your own deepening spiritual awareness into an intuitive, sensitive approach to the needs and problems of others.

✛ Monday is Gabriel's day, when his presence can most easily be sensed.

Archangel Camiel

✣ Camiel is the archangel of courage and moral strength. He is associated with the planet Mars and is also a protector of the vulnerable. A crusading angel, also known as Angel of Divine Love, in magic Camiel is sometimes pictured as a crouching leopard on a rock, but you can also visualise him as he is often depicted, with rich green wings, wearing a deep red tunic and dark green armour, and surrounded by a halo of dark ruby flames. Archangel of justice, Camiel will help you to overcome doubts and obstacles in the path of your spiritual work, including self-imposed ones. He gives you the persistence to carry on even if you are tired or feel that you are getting nowhere, and helps you to remove any personal negativity or resentments that stand in the way of the path to greater wisdom. He works to protect the innocent in war-torn lands, as well as all people who are oppressed, and endangered species of all kinds.

✣ Camiel's fragrances are peppermint and pine.

✣ Call on Camiel to help you fight your inner dragons and when you need to rid yourself of buried or bubbling anger, the cause of which may go back years to a past injustice. Ask him also to help you become less concerned with personal injustices and wrongs and more concerned with righting inequalities in the world without becoming confrontational, aggressive, negative or destructively angry.

✣ Camiel's day is Tuesday, when his presence can most easily be sensed.

Archangel Raphael

✣ Raphael, the healer and traveller archangel, is linked with the planet Mercury. He brings harmony to the world and to individuals, offering healing of all kinds. He protects children and animals, and brings guidance and sustenance to all who are lost, whether emotionally or spiritually, as well as to any traveller on a physical journey. Archangel of dawn, he is surrounded by swirling greens and yellows, and carries a staff for guiding others over difficult terrain and a large wallet which contains money to provide sustenance for those he meets on the road. Sometimes this sustenance is pictured as a fish. Raphael works to reverse technological and chemical pollution and the adverse effects of modern living. He is the archangel who will help us to develop our own innate healing abilities and will alleviate the worries of daily lives that keep us bound to the earth. Above all he is the teacher archangel, infinitely patient with our questions and encouraging us to evolve at the pace that is right for us.

✤ Raphael's fragrances are fennel and lavender.

✤ Call on Raphael for self-healing and to heal any who you know are ill or unhappy. Call on him also for developing inner harmony so that external events do not affect your moods so intensely, for learning to ask the right questions in any spiritual work and for openness to answers not only during ritual or meditation but also during everyday events, from people you meet and from the natural world.

✤ Raphael's day is Wednesday, when his presence can most easily be sensed.

Archangel Sachiel

✤ Sachiel, the divine benefactor, is the angel of charity and is associated with Jupiter. Called the Blue Angel because a deep blue and turquoise light flecked with gold emanates from him, Sachiel works constantly to better the lives of humankind, striving to improve harvests, to increase abundance and to bring prosperity, not just for a minority but for all. He also endeavours to restore run-down areas where unemployment is rife, blending new skills with traditional knowledge. His benevolence teaches us that only if we give freely to others will our own spiritual needs be met and that for every blessing we ask we must make a pledge to give practical help to others or to the planet in some way. He encourages us to read sacred literature from many cultures and to record and preserve our own experiences so that we can understand them better and our insights will not be lost.

✤ Sachiel's fragrances are sage and sandalwood.

✤ Call on Sachiel for wisdom, idealism and altruism, and for the ability to speak only when there is something worth saying, measuring words carefully so that they are just and honest. Use him also to catch glimpses of the results of long-term spiritual goals that may seem unclear or unattainable and to learn to value wisdom gained through personal experience and overcoming difficulties as the most precious gift of all.

✢ Sachiel's day is Thursday, when his presence can most easily be sensed.

Archangel Anael

✢ Anael is the archangel of new life and regeneration, and of the pure love that we feel for a partner, friends, family and pets, as well as the respect we accord all fellow human beings and every living creature. Anael is linked with the planet Venus. One of the seven angels of creation, he is called Prince of Archangels and controls kings and kingdoms, in spite of which he is an angel associated primarily with the needs of humans. He is clothed in green, with a halo of deep pink and burnished gold that radiates in all directions. Anael brings peace and joy. As archangel of fertility, he works for the restoration of natural balance, healing rainforests, bringing wildlife habitats to the city and sprouting greenery everywhere. He helps us to feel connected with people who may have different ideas or beliefs from our own and to have sympathy for their lives and needs. He is a good counter to self-absorption in private spiritual goals, directing spirituality to improving the lives and happiness of others.

✢ His fragrances are rose and vanilla.

✢ Call on Anael when you feel isolated or impatient with people, for positive interpretations and optimistic forecasts in any situation, for remaining hopeful even in negative situations or with critical or unenthusiastic people and for seeing divinity in every flower and tree.

✢ Anael's day is Friday, when his presence can most easily be sensed.

Archangel Cassiel

✢ Though sometimes called the Archangel of Tears and Solitude, Cassiel is not at all a gloomy angel. Linked with Saturn, he is the angel of compassion. Though a prince of the seventh highest heaven, he stands on the threshold of heaven and earth weeping for the sorrows of humanity and trying to alleviate them. In magic, he is pictured with a beard riding a dragon; however, you can also visualise him swathed in dark robes, with autumnal brown wings and a halo of indigo flames. Cassiel is concerned with the earthly realm. He is the archangel of balance that unifies all things: darkness and light, sorrow and joy, night and day. He also reminds us to keep our spiritual aims modest, in the knowledge that spiritual awareness is not a quick fix but takes a lifetime even partially to attain. Cassiel works for the reversal of bad fortune, as well as for conservation of all kinds, including ecological resources, natural places, history and tradition.

✢ Cassiel's fragrances are mimosa and patchouli.

✢ Call on Cassiel for a sense of perspective so that you can value small steps towards enlightenment and for the patience to persevere with spiritual work even when progress is slow or deeper significances elude you. Call on him also to help you develop inner stillness and contemplation so that you can be an oasis of calm when others panic and fret.

✢ Cassiel's day is Saturday, when his presence can most easily be sensed.

Archangel divination by automatic writing

The most successful form of archangel communication is through a form of channelling (receiving messages) called automatic writing. This is a method of transmitting higher wisdom through psychokinesis. The hand of the writer moves a pen that records quite spontaneously words coming either from an angel or, if you prefer, from the inner wisdom rooted in the most evolved part of the writer's soul. This is a very pure form of divination and is usually received in the form of teaching or inspiration to attain our ideals.

For this ritual, choose to work with the archangel whose strengths are closest to the area in which you seek enlightenment or spiritual assistance. Work in the hour after dusk, or as close to it as you can. You can then go on to work with different archangels – perhaps one each week – as each one will have messages for you. Over time, one particular archangel may become your own higher guardian.

What you need: A candle in an appropriate fragrance for the archangel you are working with, or a beeswax candle; an incense stick in an appropriate fragrance for the archangel you are working with, or traditional incense (see pages 106–9) together with a censer and charcoal (use more incense if you are working with a beeswax candle); candles for illumination; several sheets of white paper; a white envelope; a fountain pen and black ink.

✢ Light the illumination candles.

✢ If you are using traditional incense, prepare the charcoal and censer following the instructions on pages 106–9, but do not begin burning the incense until you have lit the candle.

✢ Light the perfumed or beeswax candle. If you are using stick incense, light it from the candle. If you are using traditional incense, sprinkle it onto the charcoal disk.

✢ Using the fountain pen and white paper, spontaneously write down your question. It may be a few words or it may be several pages long.

✢ When the ink is dry, place the message in white envelope, folding over the flap but not sealing it. Set the letter where candlelight will fall upon it.

✢ Sit and slowly inhale the fragrance, picturing the archangel or sensing his presence. Most people get only a hazy impression of the archangel but are filled with a sense of peace and wonder.

✢ Still working by candlelight, take a fresh piece of white paper and, allowing your mind to go blank, let your hand write an answer to your question. The words may flow as verse, as quotations from poetry, as songs or as passages of the Bible you perhaps once knew but had forgotten. They may be seemingly unconnected and include pictures or symbols. They may be like an unfolding story or the record of a dream; equally, they may be simple and direct.

✢ When you feel there is no more to say, let the ink dry and add the pages to the envelope, folding over the flap but not sealing it. Set the envelope in front of the candle once more, so that light falls on it.

✢ Do not attempt to decipher or make sense of the message but quietly breathe in the fragrance and enjoy the peace until the candle and incense are burned through.

✛ Thank the archangel and ask that you may live and work for the greatest good and with the purest intent. Sit quietly in the darkness until you are ready to switch on a small light.

✛ Open the envelope and in the lingering fragrance read the question and the answer, again without trying to analyse them.

✛ Spend the rest of the evening quietly and place the envelope under your pillow when you go to bed. You may have a significant dream, but if not, the meaning of the message will probably become clear in the light of the next day. If this does not happen, re-read the letter when you have time, lighting the archangel fragrance if possible and gently teasing out the meaning.

✛ Make a section for this particular archangel in your fragrance journal and copy the most important parts of the message into it. If you go on working with him, in time you will have your own Gabriel or Michael book of wisdom.

✛ Keep the letters in a box or drawer.

Archangel fragrances to release fear

Try this quick ritual if you ever feel alone or afraid.

What you need: 2 or 3 of your favourite archangel fragrance candles, incenses or oils; an oil burner (if you are using oils).

✛ Light the candles or incenses, or set the oil to burn in the burner.

✛ As you inhale the fragrance, visualise the archangels of your choice standing around you like sentinels of light.

CHAPTER 10
Fragrance and Magic

Throughout this book I have suggested ways of using fragrances to increase your personal power and confidence, and to bring harmony and joy into your life. In this chapter we will work with perfumes, flowers and herbs in magical rituals and ceremonies.

Perfumes, incenses and fragrant oils have always played a central role in formal ceremonial magic, establishing a connection with higher realms and beings, such as archangels (see pages 128–34), who in medieval times were summoned to do the magician's will. Perfume also traditionally purifies and empowers an altar, thus creating a protected and energised magical space in which spell-casting and ritual work can take place.

Less formal seasonal rituals, some practised in country communities right up until the time of the Second World War, were based on the flowers, herbs and fruits that were in blossom or ripe at the time of the celebrations and whose appearance in hedgerows and fields marked the progression of the year. These aromatic herbs and scented flowers were burned or scattered in circles around field boundaries or animal stalls to bring fertility to the herds and to make the sun shine and the rain fall at the right time so that the crops might grow and be plentiful.

Today we can tap into the same aromatic energies for rituals both formal and more spontaneous. What is more, with fast worldwide transport we can also work with herbs, spices and flowers that were once used only in far-off lands.

What is magic?

On pages 96–8, I described the art of visualisation using aromas. In visualisation we use imagination, a powerful psychic tool, to transfer our need from thought into reality. Ritual magic goes one stage further by systematically building a repository of energy through a series of either pre-ordained or spontaneous steps. When this accumulated force is released in a final dramatic cascade of energy, it shatters the barriers between thought and actuality and brings our desire at least within the realms of strong possibility.

The effort required to give substance to thought is also fuelled by the energetic impetus created by ritual. Fragrance, in the form of aromatic plants, candles, incense or oils, plays an important role in this, being one of the most effective methods of amplifying natural psychic energies.

Before I explain the five stages of magic so that you can create your own spells, I would like to introduce a general altar purification and empowerment ceremony.

Altar purification and empowerment

You can use this ceremony to attract specific blessings into your life. Like all magical work, it uses repetition of both words and actions to increase the energetic intensity. Fragrance is the central tool that binds together the different components of the spell (just a word for a ritual with a definite focus and goal), amplifying its energy with a life force that pulsates through all nature.

Perform this ceremony in your indoor fragrant place, as close to sunset as possible.

What you need: A beeswax, sandalwood or rose candle in a holder; an eau de cologne version of your signature or soul fragrance (see Chapter 2 and pages 92–3), or an all-purpose essence such as lavender, jasmine or rose water; 4 small dishes or ashtrays; 4 balls of cotton wool.

✛ Move the altar to a central position so that you can walk all around it.

✛ Put a dish or ashtray and a cotton wool ball at each side of the altar to represent the four cardinal directions, North, East, South and West.

✛ Place the candle in the centre of the altar and light it. Also place the fragrance in the centre of the altar – where candle wax will not drip on it.

✢ Standing on the North side of the altar facing South, pick up the bottle of fragrance, open it and, holding it in both hands, raise it to shoulder height. Inhale the scent slowly.

✢ Lowering the bottle again, use the stopper or the index finger of your power hand (the one you write with) to place a single drop of the fragrance in the centre of your brow. As you do so, say:

With fragrance I purify myself and my spiritual work. May only goodness and light guide me, for the highest purpose and with the purest intent.

✢ Now, moving clockwise, carry out the same procedure with each of the other three directions, anointing your brow and changing only the name of the direction in the chant.

✢ Now scent a cotton wool ball with a drop of the essence and set it in the small dish in the North, saying:

With fragrance I purify my altar and my spiritual work. May this fragrance grant me ... [name the blessing you seek] *if it is right to be. I ask blessings also on ...* [Ask a blessing for someone who is ill or sad, for any distressed or badly treated animals or for any place where there is conflict, poverty or disease. If you can bless someone who is critical or unfriendly towards you, the ritual will be even more powerful.]

(If you prefer, you can pour a few drops of fragrance directly into each dish instead of using the cotton wool.)

✢ Now, moving clockwise, carry out the same procedure for each direction, repeating the request and the blessing.

✢ When you have completed the final chant and blessing, blow out the candle, sending the light to the four directions.

✢ Sit quietly in the darkness, inhaling the residual fragrance, and say softly:

May blessings grow! It shall it be so! So ends this rite in peace and harmony.

Performing fragrance spells

You can carry out fragrance rituals whenever you wish; however, dawn and dusk are particularly good for magical work, being transition times when natural energies are fluid. If the need you are working for is particularly urgent or important, perform the spell in noon sunlight.

Pay attention also to the moon phase, choosing one that is suitable for the purpose of your ritual. The waxing (or increasing) moon will attract energies into your life, the full moon will facilitate any changes you seek to make, and the waning (or decreasing) moon will help to banish anything you wish to remove from your life or to take away pain and sorrow. You can find the moon phases in some local papers, in some diaries or in *Old Moore's Almanac*, which is full of other useful astrological information.

The following are the five stages that make up a fragrance spell or ritual.

One: defining the purpose and finding a fragrance

First you need to decide on the purpose of the spell or ritual. This may be immediate and very specific (for example, get £100 so the washing machine can be repaired) or longer-term and less structured (for example, to travel abroad more, or to become healthier). You can also seek strengths or gifts for other people, animals and places. (As a bonus you will often find that your own related needs will resolve themselves when you work for others – according to the magical Rule of Three, whatever you send out will come back to you threefold.)

Next you need to choose a symbol to represent your need or wish. In fragrance magic this symbol will, of course, be a fragrance of some kind, for example basil or mint for prosperity, roses for love, sage for increased mental abilities and so on. Where possible, choose seasonal fresh flowers or herbs that grow in your region – best of all in your own garden or indoor fragrant place. A living plant is very powerful because it grows after the spell, as the powers of the spell likewise gradually increase. For a venture, project or love that needs to develop slowly, use a small plant or seedling – you can transplant it if necessary.

It is possible to buy miniature indoor pot trees, which are ideal in fragrance work for very long-term purposes. For example, you could use a tiny bay tree in spells for prosperity or a pine in spells for the cleansing away of sorrow. If you need a tree for your spell but cannot use an indoor one, you can always carry out your ritual around a tree growing somewhere outdoors, for example a blossoming apple tree for health, inner beauty or any form of fertility (from starting your own company in a back room to conceiving a baby).

Two: empowering the fragrance

You can use any action to empower the fragrance, for example chanting, dancing, clapping or drumming. Alternatively, you can perform an elemental empowerment by first scattering a clockwise circle of pot pourri, dried herbs or petals around the fragrance for Earth. Then circle the fragrance clockwise with smoke spirals from an incense stick for Air. Next carefully pass a scented candle clockwise around the fragrance for Fire. Finally, sprinkle water in which petals have been soaked or flower water in a clockwise circle for Water. The circles should be over each other. If you like, you can use an appropriate elemental fragrance for each element (see pages 17–9), but this is not absolutely necessary to make the empowerment effective.

My own favourite empowerment method involves enchanting the fragrant symbol with two incense sticks chosen according to the purpose of the ritual (see pages 31–2 and 144–8). You can use two sticks of the same fragrance or combine two different aromas. For example, in a spell concerning a career move that involves risks or speculation, you might use sweet pea incense for courage and patchouli for prosperity. In ritual work outdoors, you can use the larger garden incense sticks, which create wonderful smoke circles or rings of fire in the air.

If you choose to perform your ritual outside, work on soil or a paved area for safety, and if the source of your fragrance is a tree, stand in front of it, away from overhanging branches when using incense to enchant it – or, for greater safety, use a stamping, chanting or dancing method of empowerment that does not involve fire.

Three: raising the power

This is the most active and powerful part of the spell and involves building up the speed and intensity of the action you started in stage two. You may do this by simplifying the empowering action, so, for example if you were working with the four elements, you might raise the power by using just one, perhaps scattering herbs as you dance in a circle around the fragrance. Alternatively, you might dance or clap or drum faster as you chant. You may find that the chant changes and becomes more complex. Often what seems like doggerel in the cold light of day becomes a potent method of building up the energy, as repetitive words and sounds merge and take on a life of their own. This is a naturally evolving stage of the ritual; once you are tuned in, you can just let it happen, all the while focusing in your mind and in the chant on the purpose of the ritual.

You will feel the excitement rising within you until you reach a peak of power. This feels something like a car accelerating while still stationary with the hand brake on, or like a plane accelerating down the runway just before it becomes airborne.

Four: releasing the power

This stage is the conclusion of the spell, when the energy is transferred from the fragrance out into the cosmos. This usually takes the form of a sudden, dramatic movement or sound, for example the blowing out of a candle, the extinguishing of incense or a shout of triumph, such as 'The power is free!' or 'The wish is mine!' Alternatively, you might throw herbs or flowers into the air or leap high. Again, the release occurs spontaneously when you feel that the time is right.

Five: grounding

It is important that you bring yourself back to everyday reality after your magical work. You could sit quietly, inhaling any remaining fragrance and imagining the fulfilment of your spell, or you could listen to gentle music or tend plants. Tidying up and cleaning your tools and work area can also be an effective way of grounding. Alternatively, sit on the ground and press down with your hands and feet so that you 'earth' your energies.

A basic spell-casting

If you are using a dish of dried herbs for this spell, afterwards you can put them in a good luck, health or prosperity purse to use as a talisman.

What you need: 2 incense sticks in a holder or deep metal vase, a bowl of water, a plant or flowers or a dish of dried herbs with a fragrance suitable for your purpose (see pages 144–8), a large metal tray (if you are working indoors).

✣ Light the incense sticks and place them in the holder or vase in the East of the altar. Set the bowl of water in the West.

✣ Set the plant, flowers or dried herbs in the centre of the altar (on the metal tray if you are working indoors, naming the purpose of the spell as you do so. Also name any other relevant details, such as the time-scale within which you would like a result, for example by the time the moon is next full or when the leaves fall from the trees. Be realistic about times. (If necessary you can repeat the spell at regular intervals to keep up the impetus.)

✣ Pick up an incense stick with each hand, holding it between your thumb and first finger, palms facing inwards and curved slightly downwards. Keep the sticks at an angle of about 45 degrees and a few centimetres in front of the plant so that any ash falls on the metal tray not the plant.

✣ Simultaneously move the left-hand incense stick anti-clockwise and the right-hand one clockwise to create circles in the air. As you do so, repeat the purpose of the ritual, together with the other details you have already named, as a slow, rhythmic, almost whispered chant. Be as mundane or as poetic as you wish. For example:

> Frankincense carry me, where I would wish to be, in my new home, by cherry blossom time. So I ask and it shall be!

✣ You may find that your enchantment spontaneously increases in speed, volume and intensity, but if not, deliberately increase the momentum, chanting louder and faster. The spoken chant may become a song or you may stamp your feet to the beat; however, remain in the same spot so that the incense energies are poured into the plant. Keep up an intense but always controlled rhythm, as this is the pulse of your ritual.

✦ As you move towards full power, stop spiralling the incense sticks and point them towards the sky. You will feel them pulsating. Continue chanting and stamping, still on the same spot.

✦ When you are ready, release the power into the cosmos with a final shout of the chant or such words as:

Earth, Air, Water, Fire, grant, if right, what I desire!

As you do so, plunge the two incense sticks downwards together into the bowl of water. They will give a dramatic hiss and a burst of smoke will rise (representing the release of power). Once they are extinguished, like a spent firework, be silent. This quiet time is very important both to allow the fast-moving energies to slow into gentle growth and to ground yourself so that your mind is not buzzing after the ritual.

✦ Place your hands around the flowers or herbs to transfer any remaining power from your fingertips to them and to return yourself to everyday consciousness. As you do so, whisper your chant more and more quietly until at last it fades into silence.

✦ When the burnt-down incense is cool, crumble it into a dish and bury just a pinch in the soil around the plant to signify the transfer of power. If you use good-quality incense sticks they will be pure vegetable and so will not harm the plant. If you are working with a large tree, tie a ribbon to it as a symbol of the spell continuing to weave its magic in the coming days.

✦ Finally, tidy up and spend the rest of the day or evening peacefully. You might sit quietly absorbing the different fragrances and allowing images of your happier future to float through your mind. If you carried out a daytime ritual, you might go for a walk and then begin, even in a small way, to bring the magical energies into the real world.

✦ In the days ahead, whenever you experience doubt, hold your magical plant or herbs, or touch the tree you used in the ritual and whisper the chant for a few minutes, weaving your dreams.

The magical properties of herbs, flowers and trees

The following is a list of some of the magical properties of those fragrant herbs, flowers and trees that are most potent for spell-casting and also easy to find. Use it to create your own spells.

Herb	Power
Allspice	Money, courage, luck, healing
Almond	Abundance, prosperity, love without limits
Angelica	Banishes hostility, protection, healing, visions of the future
Apple	Fertility, health, love, long life
Basil	Love, exorcism, wealth, astral travel, conquers fears of flying
Bay	Protection, psychic powers, healing, fidelity, prosperity, fertility, purification, strength, endurance
Benzoin	Purification, prosperity, attracts business, self-employment
Bergamot	Money, property, career, success
Carnation	Strength, healing, family devotion
Catnip	Cat magic, love, beauty, happiness in the home, fertility
Cedar	Healing, purification, money, protection
Chamomile	Money, quiet sleep, affection, family
Cherry	New love, divinatory abilities, fertility, good for those who have lost jobs
Cinnamon	Spirituality, success, healing powers, psychic powers, money, love, passion
Clove	Protection, banishing negativity, self-confidence, passion, love, money
Coconut	Fertility, motherhood, the flow of new life and new energies, protection against negativity – especially psychic attack
Coriander (cilantro)	Love, health, healing, for giving birth to wise and intelligent children, anti-theft and loss of money or property
Curry mint	Protection against evil and malice, prosperity
Dill	Protection, keeping the home safe from enemies and those who have envy in their hearts, money, passion, luck

Dragon's blood	Love magic, protection, dispels negativity, increases male potency
Fennel	Protection, healing, purification, courage, travel, babies and children
Fern	Rain-making, protection, luck, riches, finding hidden treasure, youthfulness, good health, travel
Freesia	Increasing trust, inner beauty, gentleness
Geranium	Fertility, health, love, protection
Ginger	Love, passion, money, success, power
Heather	Passion, loyalty, fertility, long life, rain-making, luck
Hibiscus	Passion, love, skill in divination, self-esteem
Honeysuckle	Money, psychic powers, healing, protection
Hyacinth	Happiness, love – especially family love, desire for reconciliation
Ivy	Protection, healing, married love, fidelity, breaking possessiveness
Jasmine	Passion, moon magic, money, prophetic dreams
Juniper	Protection (especially against accidents), anti-theft, love, banishing negativity, health, increases male potency, new beginnings
Lavender	Love, protection (especially of children), quiet sleep, long life, purification, happiness and peace, kindness in relationships
Lemon	New beginnings, cleansing, energy, psychic protection, improved memory, employment
Lemongrass	Repels spite, protection against snakes (reptilian and human), passion, increases psychic awareness
Lemon verbena	Purification, love, self-esteem, protects against malice
Lilac	Cleansing of negativity, domestic happiness, contacting old friends and lovers
Lily	Purity, breaking negative influences in love, peace

Lily of the valley	Increases mental abilities, happiness, restoration of joy
Lotus	Love and passion, increasing spiritual powers, inner radiance, protection, uncovering secrets
Marigold	Protection, prophetic dreams, luck in legal matters, increases psychic powers, increases love over time
Meadowsweet	Love, divination, peace, happiness, domestic protection
Melissa (lemon balm)	Love, success, healing
Mimosa	Protection, love, prophetic dreams, purification, healing
Myrrh	Protection, banishing negativity, forgiveness, overcoming grief and loss, healing, spirituality
Orange	Love, marriage, abundance, self-confidence, good luck
Parsley	Love, protection, divination, passion, purification
Passionflower	Altruism, peace, quiet sleep, friendship, passion, enduring love
Pennyroyal	Strength, protection, peace, travel, business, prevents over-tiredness
Peppermint	Money, protection while travelling, purification, energy, love, healing, increases psychic powers
Pine	Healing, fertility, purification, protection, money, returns hostility to sender
Poppy	Fertility, sleep, money, luck, invisibility in a threatening situation
Rose	Love, enchantment, increases psychic powers, healing, love and love divination, luck, protection
Rosemary	Love, passion, increases mental powers, banishes negativity and nightmares, purification, healing, quiet sleep, increases radiance and charisma, preserves youthfulness

Saffron	Love, healing, happiness, raising the winds, passion, strength, increases psychic powers, offers second sight
Sage	Long life, wisdom, protection, grants wishes, improves memory, good health, power of all kinds, leadership
Sagebrush	Purification, banishing negativity, empowerment
St John's wort	Health, power, protection, strength, love and fertility, love divination, happiness
Sandalwood	Protection, healing, banishes negativity, spirituality, contact with guardian angels/higher self
Spearmint	Healing, love, increasing memory and concentration, protection during sleep
Sweetgrass	Help with mothering issues, nurturing protection, wisdom, purification, psychic awareness
Sweet marjoram	Protection, love, happiness, health, money
Sweet pea	Friendship, purity, courage, strength
Thyme	Health, healing, prophetic dreams, increases psychic powers, improves memory, prosperity, love and love divination, purification, new jobs, courage
Valerian	Love and love divination, quiet sleep, fertility, purification, protection against hostility/inner fears/despair
Vanilla	Love, passion, increases mental acuity, fidelity, harmony
Vetivert	Love, breaking a run of bad luck, money, anti-theft, protects against all negativity
Violet	Modesty, secrecy, uncovering hidden talents, new love, love that cannot be revealed
Yerba santa	Beauty, healing, increasing psychic awareness, protection
Ylang ylang	Love, passion, sensuality, self-esteem, harmony, psychic work and meditation

CHAPTER 11
Healing with Fragrance

In Ancient Egypt it was said that the spirit or essence of each plant contained magical healing powers given by the deities. This spirit was transferred into oils, perfume essences or incense and was released when the fragrances were used. A similar view has been expressed by people in different cultures throughout the ages. In the modern world, the Gaia (Mother Earth) hypothesis proposed in the early 1970s by James Lovelock, a British biologist, states that the earth is a living entity. According to this principle, the earth has always provided and will continue to provide healing for all ills of the mind, body and psyche through the plants growing on her surface, many of which are being rediscovered by modern pharmaceutics. What is more, new species of plants are emerging to cure modern-day illnesses.

Aromatic plants and therapy

It is surely more than coincidence that many of the traditional healing plants are fragrant ones, since healing takes place on the level of the spirit and mind as well as the body, even for a physical ailment. Herbs and essential oils have been used in healing for thousands of years in cultures all over the world. In modern medicine, therapeutic aromatherapy and herbalism are now taking their rightful place alongside orthodox medical practices.

Although the therapeutic effects of essential oils have been known for millennia, the word 'aromatherapie' was coined only in 1928, by a French chemist, Henri Maurice Gattefosse, who worked in his family's perfume business. His research into the therapeutic effects of oils began as the result of an accident. An explosion in his laboratory badly burned his hand and he plunged it into the nearest cool liquid, a vat of pure lavender oil, to cool it. Not only did the intense pain ease but his hand healed very quickly and with little scarring.

On pages 155–6 and 171–80 you will find a list of the healing properties of different plants and oils, and on page 182 you will find some suggestions for books in which you can read more about the medical uses of herbs and oils. However, I would suggest that you always consult a qualified medical herbalist or aromatherapist (be aware that some who practise are not qualified) and always seek medical advice before treating yourself with home remedies, especially if you are pregnant or have a chronic medical condition. On page 180 you will find a list of plants you should not use in pregnancy or if you suffer from a pre-existing illness, but there may be others I have not mentioned. Since this book is about fragrance magic, however, I am going to concentrate on my own area of expertise: spiritual work that triggers the body's self-healing system.

The healing garden

The Celts were famed for their herb craft. Myths tell that Airmid, the Irish goddess of medicinal plants, cared for the grave of her brother Miach, and on this all the herbs of the world grew. As she cut each herb, it described its healing properties.

Healers in former times would grow their own herbs, and every convent and monastery had its medicinal garden. These were characterised by fragrant herbs, flowers and fruit trees, and because the herbs were grown, cut and dried by the healer, they were endowed with his or her special essence.

Ordinary people also had their herb patches, where they grew the ingredients for home-made lotions and potions. Even in the industrial age, when large numbers of people moved to towns for work, a small patch of back yard and later an allotment would often be cultivated.

You do not need acres of land – or, indeed, any land at all – to become a spiritual herbalist. A windowbox or the balcony of a flat can provide adequate space to grow a selection of healing herbs. And a green place, whether indoor or outdoor, naturally attracts health and healing to the home and family. Sitting among your fragrant herbs or healing flowers for a short time each day does seem to trigger the immune system, making you less susceptible to illnesses and helping your body to fight infections and viruses. All this benefit without actually ingesting any of your healing herbs!

The following flowers and herbs are particularly suitable for a healing garden. You will notice that some of them are the same as those I suggested for your protective garden, and you can easily combine the two. Healing flowers and herbs include basil, bergamot, chamomile, clary sage, dill, fennel, geranium, hyacinth, jasmine, lavender, lemon verbena, lily of the valley, marigold, meadowsweet, melissa (lemon balm), parsley, passionflower, peppermint, rose, rosemary, sage, St John's wort, thyme and violet.

Healing trees include almond, apple, bay, cherry, juniper, lemon, olive, pear, pine and orange; and in warmer climes acacia, apricot, coconut, fig and peach. The size of the tree is irrelevant; your tiny tub olive will become a focus of healing as well as a bringer of peace to the home.

Bury your illness and grow better health

As well as using their plants for medicinal brews, our wise great-grandmothers also had special areas of the garden where the herbs and flowers were trimmed but never picked. Here they buried illnesses symbolically and grew better health for individuals.

I remember as a little girl going to the house of a distant Irish cousin in Birmingham. Aunty Bridget, as I called her, had parts of her small garden marked off by canes with small red ribbons. Eavesdropping on the adult conversation, I learned that the lavender plant was for Mrs O'Leary, who was having her first baby after many years. The new rose bush was for another neighbour who had a bad skin complaint, and a mint not doing very well was for the old man next door who was going to have an operation on his stomach. Aunty Bridget was going plant another mint next to the ailing one so that the man would have good health by the day of his operation. In spite of my mother's glares and prods, I asked Aunty Bridget about her special garden, and she told me that she had buried animal bones with the person's name scratched on them under each plant. She told me it was something her mother had done in Ireland.

In recent years I have heard more about these magical healing patches from some older women I met in Sweden, who recalled a similar tradition. I now have my own ever-increasing patch of garden for growing health. Being squeamish, I bury stones rather than bones beneath the healing herbs and flowers. You don't need a lot of room to grow health in this way – a balcony or a few pots indoors will suffice. You can even have a healing plant at work – if for example you get a lot of work-related headaches. Alternatively, give a healing plant to a stressed colleague. Place it near his or her desk with your good wishes.

I used this healing technique on a UK television programme to help a man who had been stabbed through the heart and had recovered physically but not emotionally. He drew a heart pierced by a knife on a stone and buried it beneath a lavender bush. As the fragrant herb grew, he smelled it every day, and his grief for that part of himself that he felt had died in the attack began to ebb away.

As with many forms of healing, relief from pain or illness and the infusion of new energies are closely entwined. The fragrant growing plant is vital to replace the sickness and prevent old doubts or exhaustion from creeping back.

Spiritual healing can work even if the sick person does not know he or she is being healed. Medical research in San Francisco in the 1980s found that patients who were prayed for after heart attacks had significantly fewer heart attacks or strokes while in hospital and recovered better than a control group who were not prayed for, even though the people involved did not know prayers were being said on their behalf. In place of a prayer, some healers send a fragrant pot herb or flower to the sick (or sad) person as a gift.

To bury an illness and grow new health

This form of spiritual healing can be helpful for people suffering chronic pain, those who are recovering from an illness such as a virus that has lingered for months, or those who have undergone prolonged medical intervention involving strong drugs or surgery. It is also effective against exhaustion and depression. You can work for a friend or family member even in their absence, sending love every time you water or tend the plant. Of course, the person you are working for should continue with conventional or homeopathic treatment. Always seek medical advice from a properly qualified practitioner for an acute condition or if a baby, child or elderly person is ill for more than a few hours or if their condition seems to be deteriorating.

If the removal of pain or sorrow is the main emphasis of your healing, work during the waning moon cycle. If the infusion of new energies is the priority, work while the moon is waxing. Ten in the evening is the traditional healing hour. Work by torchlight or use a garden candle, taking care to extinguish it when you have finished your healing.

Choose a herb or flower to work with that represents relief of the condition you wish to heal, for example fennel for stomach problems or a rose bush for skin allergies (see the lists on pages 155–6 and 171–80). You can choose either to work with an established herb or flower in the garden or you can plant a new one. New plants work best if a massive infusion of energy or healing power is needed; however, if you have a particularly fast-growing or healthy plant already established, this can also give a running start to healing if the problem is a difficult one or the person you are working for is very depressed. Use seeds or saplings if you know a problem is going to take a long time to resolve; conversely, plant a herb or flower that is already in bud if you need fast relief. For a really major enterprise in healing, for instance for someone who is undergoing a lot of difficult and draining treatment, use a fragrant tree, such as bay, cedar, pine or mimosa, tying a red ribbon on a branch. If you choose a tree in a woodland or arboretum, you can expand your healing area if necessary. For a very serious illness or where you are working to ease an inevitable passing into death, use a dark crystal such as Apache tear or smoky quartz to name the purpose of the healing. Bury it beneath lavender or rose without engraving anything on it so that the cosmos or God/the Goddess will do what is best.

You can also send healing to a place or endangered species. If pollution is the problem, you might use a herb good for coughs, such as marigold. If in doubt about which herb to use for healing, pass your pendulum over the list on pages 155–6 and ask that it pull down over the most suitable one (see page 128 for more on using a pendulum).

Under the cosmic laws of return, the more healing you do for others with nature's fragrance, the more plants will energise and harmonise your own body and mind.

What you need: Enough moveable sticks and red ribbon to mark out the area of balcony, pots or garden you are going to use (the red ribbon will be knotted on each stick three times); red stickers as an alternative to sticks and ribbons if you are working with pots; white pebbles, small animal bones or crystals (rose quartz or pale amethyst will absorb most sorrows or pains, and the traditional gardener's crystals, jade, moss agate and tree agate are also good); a marker pen or implement for scratching the stone, bone or crystal; an appropriate fragrant plant to work with.

✢ Mark out an ongoing healing area in your garden with the moveable sticks. Knot a length of red ribbon three times around each marker stick. You can increase or decrease the area as you need. If you are using a balcony or indoor pots, mark the pots or planters with a ribboned stick or use a red sticker – especially useful if you are short of space and have to mix healing plants with ordinary ones. You can transplant the healing plants into larger pots as necessary or send the pot plant to the sick person as a gift.

✢ Now define the purpose of the healing.

✢ Scratch or write the purpose on the stone, bone or crystal in a marker pen (it does not matter if the words fade). You can use one or two words, for example 'remove pain', 'stop binge-eating' or 'relieve allergies', or you can use an image, for example jagged lines to represent frequent migraines. (Alternatively, you could bury an actual representation of an addiction, for example a cigarette or a sugary food that provokes a binge.)

✢ Make a hole in the soil around your chosen plant. Bury the bone, stone or crystal in the hole, as you do so naming what is being buried and, if you wish, asking for healing from God, the Goddess, your favourite deity or angel, or the universe.

✢ Fill in the hole and water the plant, picturing Mother Earth absorbing the pain or problem you are working with and asking that new life and growth fill the sick person with healing and hope. Name the specific energies you wish to grow, for example peace of mind, speedy wound healing, tranquil sleep or the restoration of vitality. State also the desired time scale, adding 'if it is right to be', for there may be factors involved that we do not understand.

✢ Make a note of ongoing healing projects in a special page of your journal so you can check on the individual plants regularly and make sure they are well tended.

Herbs, flowers and trees for healing

Anger/irritability	Chamomile, lavender, melissa, peppermint, rose
Anxiety	Bergamot, chamomile, hyacinth, lemon, lemon verbena, passionflower, sage, thyme
Arthritis/ rheumatism	Chamomile, juniper, meadowsweet, rosemary, pine, sweet marjoram
Asthma	Bergamot, lavender, lemon, lily of the valley, pine, sage, sweet marjoram
Blood Pressure (high)	Lavender, lily of the valley, melissa (lemon balm), rose
Burns	Chamomile, lavender, geranium, marigold, rose, rosemary
Circulation (poor)	Lemon, orange, rose, rosemary, thyme
Colds and influenza	Lavender, lemon, peppermint, pine, thyme, violet
Coughs, bronchitis and lung problems	Basil, bergamot, lavender, lemon, marigold, peppermint, thyme, violet
Depression	Apple blossom, basil, clary sage, geranium, jasmine, orange, St John's wort
Exhaustion	Basil, bergamot, fennel, lavender, lemon, orange, rosemary
Guilt, grief, regrets	Chamomile, jasmine, hyacinth, lavender, lily of the valley, pine, rose, sweet marjoram
Headache/ migraines	Basil, chamomile, lavender, mint, peppermint rosemary, sage
Insomnia	Clary sage, chamomile, hyacinth, lavender, orange, rose, sweet marjoram

Kidney/ bladder problems	Clary sage, juniper, parsley,
Liver and gall bladder problems	Chamomile, dill, fennel, meadowsweet, peppermint, rose, rosemary
Menopausal problems	Chamomile, clary sage, fennel, jasmine, orange, rose, St John's wort
Menstrual problems (absent/painful)	Clary sage, fennel, marigold, rose, rosemary
Menstrual problems (excessive)	Chamomile, lemon, peppermint
Panic/phobias	Basil, clary sage, lavender, passionflower, rose
PMT	Chamomile, clary sage, lavender, rosemary
Skin allergies/ rashes	Chamomile, geranium, lavender, marigold, rose, rosemary, violet
Stomach and digestive disorders	Bay, chamomile, dill, fennel, melissa (lemon balm), peppermint
Stress	Basil, bergamot, clary sage, lavender, orange, rose
Throat problems	Bergamot, lavender, lemon, marigold, sage, thyme
Toothache/mouth problems	Lavender, peppermint, thyme
Wounds/ operations	Lavender, olive, rosewood, St John' s wort, thyme

Absorbing the scent of healing herbs, flowers and trees

Another powerful personal healing technique is to absorb the living energies of herbs, flowers and trees by breathing in their fragrance, or touching a stem, branch or flower. By this method the plant transmits its healing essence through its aura or psychic energy field. These plant auras have been photographically recorded. (Where a leaf has been ripped or cut from the plant, part of the aura is missing.)

You may find that certain plants always work for you whatever your problem. These are usually all-purpose healers such as roses, lavender or sage. (This may be the origin of the mediaeval saying, 'Why should a man die when he has sage in his garden.') Alternatively, there may be a particularly fragrant tree in the local park that invariably soothes and uplifts you whether you have a queasy stomach, a migraine or a raging sore throat.

Of course, you can also draw fragrant healing from exotic flowers in hot houses or botanical gardens. My own local botanical garden, in Ventnor, Isle of Wight, has fragrant Australian, New Zealand and Mediterranean gardens as well as South African and Asian plants in the huge greenhouse. Holidays in other lands also offer opportunities to absorb the living fragrances of those exotic blooms you have so far met only as oils. You can store their healing powers against the coldest winter ills back home (or vice versa if you live in a hot country and get a chance to smell the flowers in more temperate zones).

Plant psychometry and healing

Whether at home, in the park or on holiday, intuition is vital in guiding you to the specific flower, herb or fragrant tree you need to ease a particular problem. If you later look up the medicinal properties of your chosen flower or herb in a herbal or aromatherapy dictionary, you will almost inevitably discover that you instinctively went to the right source of healing. This is not a strange or a spooky ability. Animals also *know* which plant will heal them. Our ancestors used their intuitive sense much more actively in the gathering of healing remedies. We have pushed this natural human ability into the background as medicine has become a matter of highly formulated pills prescribed by an expert. The more time you spend walking in beautiful gardens or in the countryside smelling flowers and herbs and touching trees, the more in tune with this innate power you will become.

Flowers are especially good for this form of healing because of their sweet fragrance and bright colours. Touching a flower as you inhale its fragrance is one of the most instant forms of spiritual healing. As you place your palms or fingertips on it to absorb its healing energies, you are calling upon another innate psychic power that all humans possess – psychometry, or psychic touch.

How does plant psychometry work? You are attracted intuitively to a particular plant because its unique energy pattern or blueprint (which all living things have) will put back into harmony the energy vibrations within you that are disturbed or out of synch. This dis-ease within you may be manifest as a physical symptom or as negative feelings.

If you are uncertain which flower or herb you need at any time, try holding a crystal pendulum over several different kinds and colours. When the pendulum tugs downwards and feels heavy, you have found the plant that best will heal, calm or energise you at this point in your life. The pendulum is just the external expression of your intuition or inner voice and is a good way of getting in touch with your instincts if you are out of practice.

Using plant psychometry

What you need: A living plant or plants to which you are drawn for healing.

✤ Once you have identified your healing plant, make physical contact with it, by sitting facing it and holding the stem or bark or touching the petals very lightly with your palms or fingertips. Palms are more responsive to spiritual energies because there are chakras there. Alternatively, you can create a circuit by touching two plants so that the energy flows between you and them. The more fragrant the plant, the more instant will be the connection and the more potent the healing energies transmitted.

✤ Maintaining physical contact, look at your plant and imagine its aura or psychic energy field of colour expanding to fill your vision.

✤ Take a deep breath in through your nose and slowly and gently draw the fragrance (which you can visualise as the colour of the flower or herb) entering your body and flowing round it as coloured light.

✤ Now, equally slowly and gently, breathe out through your mouth as though sighing, allowing any tension, sorrow or specific symptoms to flow out as a dark stream of mist to be absorbed by the earth.

✤ Carry on breathing in this way, establishing a regular rhythm. The fragrance will intensify as you draw the spiritual essence into yourself.

✤ When your body feels light and relaxed and your mind is calm, you have finished your healing work. In your mind's eye, the exhaled breaths will also have gradually changed to the colour of the flower.

✤ Let go of the flower, herb or tree and sit quietly picturing the coloured fragrant light, still pulsating like a well-tuned engine, at rest within you.

✤ When you are ready, get up and walk quietly among the flower or herb beds, or in the aromatic woods for a while, still enclosed inwardly in the healing light.

✤ Do something positive, however small, for the natural world to pay for the energy you have taken.

✤ If a plant works well, try its incense, oil or perfume form, perhaps making your own healing flower water (see pages 35–8) to inhale or splash on when you are tired or stressed.

CHAPTER 12
Fragrance and Love

Flowers and perfumes form an obvious focus for love and fidelity magic, and have been involved in love ritual since time immemorial. Brides in Ancient Rome wore roses as a head-dress to symbolise eternal love. In Ancient Greece, the sacred marriage of the Father God Zeus to Hera was celebrated in January, as new flowers began to bud and the trees to blossom. Hera, as well as being the chief Mother Goddess, guardian of fertility, marriage and childbirth, was also goddess of flowers. Her statues were decked with lilies, a flower that became part of the bridal bouquet or head-dress throughout western Europe and the Mediterranean.

In Mediterranean lands orange blossom was also worn as a fertility token, a custom that came from the Middle East and spread to northern and western Europe, surviving until after the Second World War. Preserved white orange blossom buds, still aromatic, were added to the bridal circlet and after the wedding were wrapped in waxed paper. The circlet was given to the bride's eldest daughter on her wedding day.

Poetry through the ages has celebrated the power of flowers and herbs to induce love. An Egyptian love poem written more than 3,000 years ago and recorded in the Papyrus of Turin, includes such lines as:

> *I am to thee like a garden,*
> *which I have planted with flowers*
> *and with all manner of sweet smelling herbs.*
> *My heart is satisfied with joy ...*
> *Because we walk together.*

I found this translation, by Aylward M Blackman, in an out-of print book by Adolf Erman called *The Love Poetry and Prose of Ancient Egypt* (Dover Press, 1955).

The Elizabethan poet Christopher Marlowe (1564–93), wrote in 'The Passionate Shepherd to his Love':

And I will make thee beds of roses,
And a thousand fragrant posies
A cap of flowers and a kirtle
Embroidered all with leaves of myrtle.

Folklore is also full of fragrant flowers and herbs to attract love and fertility. According to tradition, a woman wishing to become pregnant should pick the yellow herb St John's wort at midnight on Midsummer's Eve (the time of year when it first blooms). She should walk naked and alone in the garden without speaking a word. She must then sleep with the plant under her pillow. However, there was competition for the herb. Maidens seeking a husband would also gather St John's wort after dusk on Midsummer's Eve, having eaten nothing all day. It was said they would be married before the year was out. If the maiden slept with the yellow plant under her pillow, she was promised dreams of her true love, known or as yet unknown.

Roses

Roses are a symbol of love in almost every culture and a potent ingredient in much love magic.

Roses in the language of flowers

Though in fact thousands of years old, the language of flowers was first formalised in the early eighteenth century by Lady Mary Wortley Montagu, wife of the English ambassador to Turkey. It was popularised by the Victorians. According to this catalogue of flower symbolism, rosebuds are a symbol of a first or new love, the blossoming rose is a symbol of passion and commitment, and the full-blown rose a symbol of love in maturity. Different colours also have different meanings. A pink rose, for example, indicates new love or a lover afraid to show his or her feelings. A red rose says, 'I love you.' A fragrant wild rose represents more uncertain affection: 'I love you from afar,' while a yellow rose says, 'I am jealous.'

Even the way the rose was given to a lover was full of significance. A single rose on a plain stem offered flower uppermost expressed positive feelings and intentions on the part of the donor. A rosebud surrounded by thorns and leaves and given to the would-be lover upright conveyed uncertainty that love was returned. If the recipient inverted the rosebud and handed it back, he or she was equally uncertain but not entirely rejecting the overture. If the lover removed the thorns and returned the rosebud upright, there was true feeling. However, if the rosebud was returned with the leaves removed, there was no hope of the love progressing.

Rose love spells

Most spells to attract a lover (either known or unknown) use pink or fragrant red roses. Roses in full bloom are increasingly being used magically by optimistic lovers second or third time around.

Rose-burning spells

Many traditional folk rituals for love involve burning petals in a candle flame. The idea is that the energy created by the burning petals acts as the catalyst to draw a hesitant or as yet unknown lover into the telepathic, and hopefully soon afterwards physical, sphere of the spell-caster. Of course, there is the not so insignificant business of free will and compatibility to take into account, and an unwilling lover, whether held by magic or by earthly means, rarely brings happiness. Nevertheless, in my own experience rose-burning spells work well not only for young girls but also for divorced and older people who are looking for love, perhaps after a period alone.

Indeed, last time I went to a festival in Malmö, southern Sweden, I got through two huge vases of roses in two days, and a lot of very romantically empowered people went off radiating confidence and charisma, hopeful that they could and would find the right person. After burning their petals, some decided to ask a work colleague with whom they had become friendly out on a date, others to demand that a half-hearted lover either show commitment or leave the stage. One lady in her mid-eighties hurried away to her warden-assisted apartment by the sea clutching her burned petals and eager to ask the old gentlemen in the next flat to come on the weekly ferry bus trip to Copenhagen with her.

Rose candle spell to call love into your life or increase affection

This is my favourite rose candle spell. Begin it at midnight on the night of the crescent moon for an unknown love, or on any night up to the full moon for an existing friendship or a relationship you would like to become more intense. The closer to the full moon, the more powerful the energies for increasing the pace of the relationship. You could use the waning moon for removing obstacles in the way of love.

You will need: A large rose or rosebud with petals that are quite dry but not brown (use pink for love not yet found or at the friendship stage, red for putting impetus into a slow-moving relationship or for marriage, and yellow if you have loved and lost and would like to love again); a small squat beeswax or rose-scented candle; a deep wide-based candleholder broad enough to catch a pool of melted wax, or a metal tray with sides, or a ceramic dish to put under the candle; a small ceramic or metal dish to hold burning petals; sugar tongs (optional); a tall slender vase; a paper knife, small screwdriver or awl; a sharp knife for cutting wax; a piece of pink silk; some dried or fresh rose petals.

✢ Light the candle, as you do so saying:

*I light this candle for my love. Far or near, known or hidden
from my sight, I wish to see my love this night.*

✢ If you are using a tray or dish, drip a little wax onto it to hold the candle firm, then place the candle in the holder, tray or dish.

✢ Take a small petal from the rose and, holding it between your index finger and thumb or using the sugar tongs, carefully singe a corner of it in the candle flame.

✢ Drop the burning petal into the small dish, making sure the dish is not too near the candle – candles are quite volatile and the petal might flare up, causing a fire. It doesn't matter if the petal burns completely or goes out. As it burns, say:

*I burn this petal for my love. Burn, rose, burn heart with love.
Far or near, known or hidden from my sight, I ask to see my
love this night.*

✤ Burn a second petal in the same way and set it also in the dish, saying as you do so:

> *I burn this petal for my love. Burn, rose, burn love in me this hour. I call my love in flame and flower.*

✤ Burn a third and final petal and drop that in the dish, saying as you do so:

> *I burn this petal for my love. Burn rose, burn flame within us of desire. My love appears in candle fire.*

✤ Hold the rose from which you have plucked the petals and, looking into the candle flame, picture a misty figure moving towards you out of the light. Close your eyes, blink and in the aura around the flame or in your mind's eye you may see, momentarily, a face. It may be the face of your present love or, if you are not in a relationship, it may be the face of an unknown person yet to come into your life or of someone you think of as a friend or colleague but who could, if you wish, become much more. If the mists do not clear, the time is not right for you to know the identity of your lover. Be patient, for the face may come to you in a dream. In the meantime focus on other areas of your life, knowing that love will come when you least expect it. If you are already in a relationship and the mists do not clear, it is not a bad omen but rather a reflection of uncertainties you may not have voiced even to yourself, or of a need for greater commitment on one or both sides. These issues need talking through.

✤ When the candle has melted, press the burned petals into the remaining pool of wax and mark a heart shape around them with the paper knife, small screwdriver or awl.

✤ When the wax is set, using the sharp knife carefully cut out the heart with the petals embedded in it and wrap it in the pink silk with the dried or fresh rose petals. Keep it in a drawer until your love comes or the wax crumbles, in which case repeat the spell.

To consummate love or increase passion in an established relationship

This ritual should be carried out alone before love-making. It can also be used before an important date or a non-sexual milestone in a relationship or when you need a massive infusion of confidence to get back into the social scene after a break-up or a period alone. I have also known women who have conceived after using this spell before love-making.

The ritual makes use of your signature fragrance. As we noted in Chapter 2, your signature fragrance defines you and makes you feel special in every way. You may have been wearing it when you first met your partner or when you consummated your love, or you may have bought it for your wedding and honeymoon. It is therefore an excellent focus for this ritual, whether you are making love for the first time or restoring passion to a relationship that has become bogged down in earthly demands. The ritual also makes use of the seven chakras (see pages 62–9), focusing on endowing your signature fragrance and yourself with the seven natural forces manifest in the chakras.

The real magic of this ritual lies in making time for yourself to get in touch with and enjoy your own sensual feelings. Various surveys over the last few years have indicated that many modern women prefer to go to bed with a good book, and if love-making is always fitted in at the end of a long day before another equally long day, this is not surprising. You could wait for a special occasion when you are having a romantic overnight break in a hotel to perform this ritual. Alternatively, with a little stage management you can banish flatmates, children and pets for the evening, dedicating this time to love and sensuality.

In time, if you have a sensitive lover, he or she may enjoy being present during the chakra ritual and can anoint you while you weave joint empowerments. The words of the ritual, as of all the others in the book, are just suggestions, so change and adapt them as necessary. If you like, you can use your partner's favourite cologne to anoint his or her chakras and visualise the rainbow colours enfolding you both as you make love or lie quietly, talking of your future together.

What you need: 10 drops of fragrant love essential oil (such as jasmine, mimosa, rose or ylang ylang) and a cup of full-fat milk or 30 ml/1 tbsp sweet almond oil, or a commercially scented bath milk; a rose-scented candle; rose quartz crystals or pink glass nuggets; a bottle of your signature perfume; 4 small scented candles in jasmine, rose, sandalwood or ylang ylang (or one of each if you prefer) and suitable holders; scented candles of your choice for illumination and suitable holders.

✣ About an hour before you know your lover will arrive at your house or come to bed, take the rose-scented candle to the bathroom and light it. Run yourself a bath using the fragrant love oil and milk or almond oil, or the commercially scented bath milk.

✣ Get in the bath, swirl the light pools and drop the rose quartz crystals or glass nuggets one by one into the water, making an empowering statement about yourself for each one. Visualise the scented crystalline light shimmering around your body and clear your mind of all thoughts of work, family or finances, allowing them to dissolve in the light pools.

✣ When you are ready, get out, dry yourself and put on a loose robe that opens down the front, swirling any final doubts or negativity down the plughole with the bath water. Focus on the shimmering perfumed crystalline light within you as you move into your bedroom.

✣ Light the illumination candles and the four small candles and place them in holders. Put the small candles in the four corners of the room. Open your signature fragrance and set it on a flat surface.

✣ You are now going to work with the base chakra. This is the chakra of the earth and of pure instinctual power. It will help you shed inhibitions and tune into the seasonal flow of earth energy, in which sexuality is one of the natural forces, celebrated in ancient fertility festivals to bring new life to the world. Put your hands on the small of your back and press to awaken the Kundalini – the serpent power named after a Hindu love goddess that is coiled round the base of the spine. With your signature fragrance anoint the small of your back or the soles of your feet (where the earth energy enters your body as you walk), saying:

I am the earth and I take into myself my own power. Earth pulsate within me.

Picture the rich red light of the sleeping serpent love goddess awakening your body and flowing upwards, warming and energising you with animal sensuality so that your body responds instinctively and spontaneously to your lover's touch.

✣ Move upwards to the sacral chakra. This is the chakra of the moon, of water and of pure lust – the hunger to merge your body with that of your lover physically and emotionally. Press gently just below your navel to locate this source of warm and powerful desire. Taking your signature fragrance, anoint the area below your navel with a single drop, gently massaging it in circles and saying:

I am the Moon and the flowing waters. I take into myself my own power. Moonlight radiate within me, water flow.

Visualise spheres of silver brilliance flowing upwards and downwards, merging with the base chakra's red and connecting you with the ebbs and flows of desire within your body and mind.

✣ Move upwards to the solar plexus chakra. This is the chakra of the sun and of fire. It represents your power and confidence to reach out for the person you want and the certainty that you are not choosing this person as your mate out of fear of loneliness or gratitude that someone could love you. Gently touch the area in the centre of your stomach between your navel and your breasts. Anoint your solar plexus with your signature fragrance, saying:

I am the sun. I am pure fire and I take within myself my own power. Sun and fire burn bright within me.

Visualise clear yellow rays of light like morning sunshine radiating from this area, pulsating upwards and downwards and merging with red and silver. They fill you with the self-love and self-esteem without which you cannot reach out to another.

✣ Move upwards to your heart chakra. This is the chakra of the winds, the joining of the fierce wind of the North, the challenging wind of the East, the cherishing wind of the South and the rain-bringing wind of the West that washes away fears and uncertainty. This chakra gives you the power to connect heart to heart, allowing the boundaries of the separate self to dissolve in the safety of mutual love and respect. Touch the area between your breasts and anoint it with your signature fragrance (or, if you prefer, anoint the palm of each hand) saying:

I am the winds and I take within myself my own power. Swirling winds carry me from separate love to unity.

Picture rich green swirls of mist moving upwards and downwards within you, joining with the red, silver and yellow light within. Know that you will care for the other's feelings even in the midst of the most intense love-making.

✦ Move upwards to the throat chakra. This is the chakra of sound, from which are spoken words of truth from the heart rather than the mind and from which flows honesty in all matters. Gently touch the centre of your throat. Now anoint it with your signature fragrance, saying:

> *I am pure sound and I take within myself my own power. May neither secrets nor coldness destroy the words of love that flow between us.*

Picture deep sky-blue light spiralling within you upwards and downwards, merging with the green, red, silver and yellow. Vow to yourself that you will never let the day end in anger or indifference between you and your lover.

✦ Move upwards to your brow chakra. This is the chakra of pure light, the union of two souls and spirits as well as heart, body and mind. With the psychic and spiritual union, love-making ceases to be primarily physical and moves into a higher plane of experience, sometimes giving rise to an out of body experience. Touch the centre of your brow just above and between your eyes. Anoint the chakra, saying:

> *I am pure light and I take within myself my own power. May we walk in the light of love to deep and lasting understanding.*

Visualise rich turquoise or indigo/purple light flowing upwards and downwards within you and merging with the blue, green, red, silver and yellow.

✦ Move upwards to the crown chakra – the most significant in love and love-making. The is the chakra of unity, the point at which true spiritual bliss, unity with your lover and maybe momentarily with the cosmos may be expressed and experienced in sexual orgasm. Touch the centre of your hair line. Anoint the chakra, saying:

> *I am as one with my lover and through our love with the universe. I take within myself this power. Let this union be*

blessed in whatever way is right to be, and may we love till the sun no longer turns and the seas run dry.

Visualise rich violet or pure white light flowing from you and enclosing your lover wherever he or she is waiting.

✤ Light the scented candles in the bedroom and anoint the sheets with your signature fragrance. Wait quietly for your lover to come to you.

✤ As you make love, recall the powers you carry within you and enfold your lover in the certainty and trust of your mutual love.

Afterword

It is early morning, after rain, and the garden is filled with perfume.

Last night I went to bed not like Marilyn Monroe, with my dream lover and wearing only my signature fragrance, but hugging my microwavable lavender pillow, and sprinkling eucalyptus (rather than rose petals) around the bed to stave off a summer cold.

Before late-rising teenagers come hammering on the bathroom door, I will run myself a bath, pouring some of my home-made Summer Solstice rose and rosemary cologne into the water to fill me with enthusiasm and energy for the challenges the day has to offer. I left this cologne in the garden from dawn to noon on the longest day to fill it with sun power. Afterwards I will splash on the last drops of my signature fragrance, Arpège.

Fragrance magic is sometimes ethereal and beautiful, filled with lavender fields, rose gardens and moments of love and illumination as we finally encounter our guardian angel or are carried into a past world by an exotic essence. But perfume is also, as it always has been, a part of the everyday world, uplifting, reassuring and giving the confidence to get out there and succeed against all odds when the body is begging to be allowed to stay under the duvet.

Fragrance is precious whether in the form of a few flowers picked from the garden as a gift by a small child or the most splendid bouquet sent by a lover on a special anniversary. Whenever we smell a rose or fill a herb sachet, we are joining with people in different lands across thousands of years who have carried out similar actions in hope and in confidence that all shall be well. If you are sad or worried, spend a little time in the park or your garden or the nearest hothouse. Even in the winter, there you will find aromas to lift your heart and spirit.

I may even light my rose candle tonight and burn a large pile of rose petals to call a wealthy lover from the cosmic dating pool to my door to share my microwaveable pillow.

Fragrant Correspondences

F = flower, P = perfume, S = signature fragrance, H = herb, O = oil, I = incense, Sm = smudge

Fragrance	Latin name and form	Healing properties	Magical properties	Planet
Agrimony	*Agrimonia eupatoria* H	Cuts and bruises, liver/bladder problems, stomach/digestive disorders, throat problems	Protective, banishes negative energies	Jupiter
Alchimie (Rochas)	N/A P, S	Includes: bergamot, jasmine, passionflower, vanilla		N/A
Alexandra (Alexandra de Markoff)	N/A P, S	Includes: marigold, jasmine, rose, patchouli, vetivert		N/A
Aliage (Estée Lauder)	N/A P, S	Includes: citrus, jasmine, pine, thyme, musk, vetivert, myrrh		N/A
Amarige (Givenchy)	N/A P, S	Includes: violet leaves, ylang ylang, musk, vanilla		N/A
Amazone (Hermès)	N/A P, S	Includes: violet leaves, hyacinth, blackcurrant, jasmine, lily of the valley, vetivert, ylang ylang		N/A
Amour Amour (Jean Patou)	N/A P, S	Includes: bergamot, lemon, jasmine, rose, ylang ylang, carnation, lily, vetivert, musk		N/A
Anais Anais (Cacharel)	N/A P, S	Includes: lily, blackcurrant bud, hyacinth, lily of the valley, jasmine, rose, ylang ylang, vetivert, musk		N/A
Angelica	*Angelica archangelica* H, O	Colds/respiratory problems, colic, flatulence, heartburn, liver problems, menstrual cramps	Banishes hostility, protective, visions of the future	Sun
Apple blossom	*Pyrus* I, H	Depression, general health, fertility	Relationships, abundance love, youthfulness, fertility, optimism	Venus
Arpège (Lanvin)	N/A P, S	Includes: bergamot, rose, jasmine, ylang ylang, lily of the valley, vetivert, vanilla, musk		N/A
Basil	*Ocymum Basilicum* H, O, I	Coughs/bronchitis/lung problems, depression, exhaustion, headaches/migraines, panic/phobias, stress	Fidelity, prosperity, astral projection, counters fears of flying, protection	Mars
Bay	*Laurus nobilis* H, O, Sm	Stomach/digestive disorders	Healing, prosperity, fidelity, domestic protection, marriage	Sun

Fragrance	Latin name and form	Healing properties	Magical properties	Planet
Beautiful (Estée Lauder)	N/A P, S	Includes: bergamot, lemon, rose, ylang yang, violet, lilac, lily of the valley, carnation, sage, geranium, chamomile, vetivert, vanilla, musk		N/A
Bergamot	Citrus bergamia H, O, I	Anxiety, asthma, coughs/bronchitis/ lung problems, exhaustion, stress, throat problems	Prosperity, career, success, property	Mercury
Birch	Betula pendula H, O	Arthritis/rheumatism, cellulite, dry skin/ dandruff, kidney problems, PMT	Cleansing, healing, new beginnings, protection, wisdom	Venus
Byzance (Rochas)	N/A P, S	Includes: basil, jasmine, lily of the valley, ylang ylang, vanilla, musk		N/A
Cabotine (Gres)	N/A P, S	Includes: ylang ylang, lily, hyacinth, rose, carnation, jasmine, blackcurrant bud, vanilla, musk, vetivert		N/A
Capricci (Nina Ricci)	N/A P, S	Includes: bergamot, rose, hyacinth, jasmine, ylang ylang, lily of the valley, vetivert, musk		N/A
Carnation	Dianthus carophyllus F, P, I, O, soul fragrance	Energy and restoration of strength during convalescence, calming in times of stress	Happiness, healing, family devotion protection, strength	Sun
Cedar/ cedarwood	Cedrus libani H, O, I, Sm	Bladder problems, respiratory problems, skin complaints, stress	Cleansing of negative/ redundant thoughts, healing, prosperity, protection, purification	Sun
Chamomile	Chamaemelum nobile F, I, H, O, soul fragrance	Anger/irritability, anxiety arthritis/rheumatism, headaches/migraines, insomnia, liver/gall bladder problems, menopausal problems, excessive menstrual bleeding, PMT, skin allergies/rashes, stomach/digestive disorders	Affection, family, prosperity, quiet sleep, all matters concerning babies and children	Sun
Chanel No. 5	N/A P, S	Includes: jasmine, rose, ylang ylang		N/A
Chloe (Karl Lagerfeld)	N/A P, S	Includes: honeysuckle, ylang ylang, hyacinth, lilac, jasmine, rose		N/A
Cinnabar (Estée Lauder)	N/A P, S	Includes: cloves, bergamot, jasmine, rose, carnation, ylang ylang, vanilla		N/A

Fragrance	Latin name and form	Healing properties	Magical properties	Planet
Cinnamon	*Cinnamomum zeylanicum* I, O, spice	Skin disorders, colds, chills	Healing, love, passion, prosperity, psychic awareness, spirituality	Mars
Citronella Sun	*Cymbopogen nardus* I, O	Antiseptic, insect repellent, rheumatism	Protection, psychic powers, improves memory, technological ability	
Clary sage	*Salvia sclarea* H, O	Depression, insomnia, kidney/bladder problems, menopausal problems, painful or absent menses, panic/phobias, PMT, stress	Banishes negativity, overcomes fears/nightmares, spirituality, peace and reconciliation	Moon
Clove	*Syzygium aromaaticum* H, I, O, spice	Circulatory problems, memory loss, toothache	Love, money, passion, repelling hostility/envy, self-confidence, offers solace after sorrow or betrayal	Jupiter
Diamonds and Emeralds (Elizabeth Taylor)	N/A P, S	Includes: rose, sage, hyacinth, jasmine, lily of the valley, carnation, rose, lily, vanilla, musk, vetivert		N/A
Dill	*Anethum graveolens* H	Liver/gall bladder problems, stomach/digestive disorders	Love, luck, passion, prosperity, protection, repels malice/envy, travel	Mercury
Dioressence (Christian Dior)	N/A P, S	Includes: jasmine, geranium, cinnamon, carnation, ylang ylang, vetivert, vanilla, musk		N/A
Donna Karan New York	N/A P, S	Includes: lily, rose, ylang ylang, jasmine, vetivert, vanilla, musk		N/A
Eau de Cologne (Hermès)	N/A P, S	Includes: mint, lemon, bergamot, basil, lily of the valley, honeysuckle, lavender, rosemary		N/A
Elderflower Venus	*Sambucus canadensis* F, H	Arthritis/rheumatism, asthma, insomnia, respiratory problems	Health, lucky at weddings, cures nightmares, prosperity, protection from extremes of weather	
Escape (Calvin Klein)	N/A P, S	Includes: blackcurrant bud, chamomile, jasmine, rose, clove, carnation, musk		N/A
Eucalyptus	*Eucalyptus globulus* H, O, I	Asthma, bronchitis, burns, colds/coughs/influenza, cold sores, cuts, cystitis, diarrhoea, fluid retention, headaches (congestive/sinusitis), lung/respiratory problems	Aids focus/concentration, banishes negativity, purification, repels psychic attacks	Moon

Fragrance	Latin name and form	Healing properties	Magical properties	Planet
Fennel	*Foeniculum vulgare* H, O, I	Exhaustion, liver/gall bladder problems, menopausal problems, painful or absent menstruation, stomach/ digestive disorders	Courage, protection, stamina, strength	Mercury
Fern	*Dryoptens wallichiana* H, I	Not used medicinally	Good luck, healing, moving house, protection, rain-making, travel	Mercury
Fidji (Guy Laroche)	N/A P, S	Includes: hyacinth, lemon, bergamot, carnation, ylang ylang, jasmine, rose, vetivert, musk		N/A
First (Van Cleef & Arpels)	N/A P, S	Includes: blackcurrant bud, hyacinth, rose, jasmine, lily of the valley, carnation, vetivert, musk		N/A
Frankincense	*Boswellia carterii* O, I	Bronchitis, coughs/ colds/throat problems, skin disorders	Courage, joy, strength, success, ritual magic, travel, wealth	Sun
Geranium	*Pelargonium* F, H, O, I, soul fragrance	Burns, depression, skin allergies/rashes, wounds	Fertility, health, love, protection, positivity	Venus
Giorgio Beverly Hills	N/A P, S	Includes: bergamot, jasmine, rose, carnation, ylang ylang, lily of the valley, hyacinth, musk		N/A
Heather	*Calluna* F, I, H	Not used medicinally	Fertility, long life, loyalty, luck, passion, rain-making	Venus
Hibiscus	*Hibiscus* F, I, H, soul fragrance	Not used medicinally	Divination, good fortune, love, passion, lasting love and marriage, magical abilities	Venus
Histoire D'Amour (Aubusson)	N/A P, S	Includes: bergamot, basil, jasmine, rose, ylang ylang, musk		N/A
Honeysuckle	*Lonicera caprifolium* F, H, I, soul fragrance	Coughs, catarrh, asthma, stomach problems (Berries poisonous)	Healing, luck, prosperity, protection, psychic powers	Jupiter
Hyacinth	*Hyacinthus orientalis* F, H, I, soul fragrance	Anxiety, guilt/grief/ regrets, insomnia, depression, healing of cuts/wounds	Happiness, love (especially family), reconciliation, relieves nightmares	Venus
Jasmine	*Jasminum officinale* F, H, O, I, soul fragrance	Depression, guilt/grief/ regrets, menopausal problems, PMT, cramp/ aches, skin problems	Passion, moon magic, prosperity, prophetic dreams, love, psychic development	Moon
Je Reviens (Worth)	N/A P, S	Includes: bergamot, violet, clove, rose, jasmine, hyacinth, lilac, ylang, ylang, vetivert, musk		N/A

Fragrance	Latin name and form	Healing properties	Magical properties	Planet
Jolie Madame (Balmain)	N/A P, S	Includes: bergamot, jasmine, rose, vetivert, musk		N/A
Juniper	*Juniperus communis* H, O, I, Sm	Arthritis/rheumatism, kidney/bladder problems	Banishes negativity, new beginnings, healing, love, protection	Sun
KL (Karl Lagerfeld)	N/A P, S	Includes: orange, bergamot, clove, cinnamon, rose, jasmine, ylang ylang, myrrh, vanilla		N/A
L'Air du Temps (Nina Ricci)	N/A P, S	Includes: bergamot, carnation, jasmine, rose, ylang ylang, lily, clove, musk, vetivert		N/A
Laura Ashley No. 1	N/A P, S	Includes: hyacinth, bergamot, rose, jasmine, clove, carnation, musk, vanilla		N/A
Lavender	*Lavendula officienale* F, H, I, O, Sm, soul fragrance	Anger/irritability, asthma, high blood pressure, burns, colds/influenza, coughs/bronchitis/lung problems, exhaustion, guilt/grief/regrets, headaches/migraines, insomnia, panic/phobias, PMT, skin allergies/rashes, stress, throat problems, toothache/mouth problems, wounds/operations	Happiness and peace, long life, love, protection, quiet sleep	Mercury
Lemon	*Citrus limon* F, I, O	Anxiety, asthma, poor circulation, colds/influenza, coughs/bronchitis/lung problems, exhaustion, excessive menstrual flow, throat problems	Clarity, cleansing, energy, psychic protection, improved memory, new beginnings	Moon
Lemon Verbena	*Lippia citriodora* H, I, O	Anxiety, stress, insomnia	Love, purification	Mercury
Lemongrass	*Cymbopogon citratus* H, I, O	Depression, headaches	Repels spite, protection against snakes (reptilian and human), passion, lust, psychic awareness	Mercury
Lilac	*Syringa vulgaris* F, H, I, soul fragrance	Not used medicinally	Banishes negativity, domestic happiness, protection	Venus

Fragrance	Latin name and form	Healing properties	Magical properties	Planet
Lily	*Lilium* F, H, I, soul fragrance	External ulcers, skin problems, vaginal infections	Breaking negative influences in love, purification	Mercury
Lily of the valley	*Convallaria* F, I, H, soul fragrance	Asthma, high blood pressure, guilt/grief/ regrets	Increases mental abilities, happiness, restores joy	Mercury
Lime	*Tilia vulgaris* O, I	Greasy skin, arthritis, poor circulation, colds/ influenza	Health/well-being to family and home, healing, love, protection	Sun
Linden blossom	*Tilia europaea* F, I, H, O, soul fragance	High blood pressure, high cholesterol, depression	Love, luck, protection, quiet sleep	Jupiter
L'Insolent (Charles Jourdan)	N/A P, S	Includes: bergamot, jasmine, lily of the valley, carnation, musk, vanilla		N/A
Lotus	*Nymphaea lotus* F, I, P, O, soul fragrance	Soothing, calming	Love, new beginnings, passion, increasing spiritual powers, inner radiance, protection, reveals secrets	Sun/ Moon
Ma Griffe (Carven)	N/A P, S	Includes: clary sage, jasmine, rose, vetivert, ylang ylang, cinnamon, musk		N/A
Magie Noire (Lancôme)	N/A P, S	Includes: hyacinth, bergamot, jasmine, ylang ylang, lily of the valley, musk		N/A
Marigold	*Calendula officinalis* F, H, O, I, soul fragrance	Burns, coughs/bronchitis/ lung problems, absent/ painful menstruation, skin allergies/rashes, throat problems	Protection, prophetic dreams, legal matters, psychic development, love	Sun
Meadowsweet	*Spiraea filipendula* F, H, I	Arthritis/rheumatism, liver/gall bladder problems, swellings	Divination, happiness, love, peace, protection from malice	Jupiter
Melissa	*Lemon balm* H, I, O	Anger/irritablility, high blood pressure, stomach/digestive disorders	Healing, love, success	Moon
Michelle (Balenciaga)	N/A P, S	Includes: jasmine, ylang ylang, rose, carnation, musk, vetivert, vanilla		N/A
Mimosa	*Acacia dealbata* F, O, I, soul fragrance	Cuts/infected wounds, stomach upsets, stress	Protection, love, prophetic dreams, purification, healing	Saturn
Mint, garden	*Mentha* H, I, O	Headaches/migraines, digestive disorders	Money, love, increasing sexual desire, healing, banishing malevolence, protection while travelling	Venus

Fragrance	Latin name and form	Healing properties	Magical properties	Planet
Musk	Artificial P, S, I	Not used medicinally	Love, passion, inner radiance	Venus
Myrrh	Commiphora myrrha I, H, O	Teeth/gums, wounds, arthritis, skin problems, nasal/chest congestion	Protection, banishes negativity, forgiveness, grief/loss, healing, spirituality	Moon
Narcisse Noir (Caron)	N/A P, S	Includes: bergamot, lemon, rose, jasmine, musk		N/A
Norell (Revlon)	N/A P, S	Includes: carnation, hyacinth, rose, jasmine, musk		N/A
Obsession (Calvin Klein)	N/A P, S	Includes: bergamot, lemon, jasmine, rose, vanilla, musk		N/A
Oh La La! (Azzaro)	N/A P, S	Includes: bergamot, rose, jasmine, ylang ylang, cinnamon, vanilla		N/A
Opium (YSL)	N/A P, S	Includes: cloves, bay, jasmine, rose, carnation, lily of the valley, cinnamon, vetivert, myrrh, musk		N/A
Orange	Citrus sinesis F, I, O	Circulation (poor), depression, exhaustion, insomnia, menopausal problems, stress	Love, marriage, abundance, self-confidence, marriage, good luck	Sun
Orange blossom (neroli)	Citrus aurantium F, O, I	Not used medicinally	Love, fidelity, healing, marriage, fertility, childbirth	Sun/Venus
Panthère (Cartier)	N/A P, S	Includes: jasmine, rose, carnation, ylang ylang, musk, vanilla		N/A
Papyrus flower	Cyperus papyrus F, O, I, Soul fragrance	Not used medicinally	Protection, wisdom, altruism, idealism, awareness of other dimensions	Mercury
Parsley	Petrolselinium sativum H	Kidney/bladder problems, menstrual difficulties, bad breath, digestion	Love, protection, divination, passion, purification	Mercury
Passionflower	Passiflora incarnate F, I, O, soul fragrance	Anxiety, panic attacks, phobias, asthma, skin disorders, neuralgia, shingles	Sacrifice, peace, quiet sleep, friendship, passion, love forever	Venus
Patchouli	Pogostemon patchouli I, O, H	Stress, burns, skin problems/allergies, sexual dysfunction	Prosperity, lust, property, material security, fertility	Saturn

Fragrance	Latin name and form	Healing properties	Magical properties	Planet
Peppermint	*Mentha piperata* H, O, I	Anger/irritability, colds/ influenza, coughs/ bronchitis/lung problems, headaches/ migraines, liver/gall bladder problems, excessive menstrual discharge, stomach/ digestive disorders, toothache/mouth problems, travel sickness	Purification, energy, love, healing, psychic development, quiet sleep	Mercury
Pheromone (Marilyn Miglin)	N/A P, S	Includes: jasmine, wild grasses		N/A
Pine	*Pinus sylvestris* I, H, O, Sm	Arthritis/rheumatism, asthma, colds/influenza	Healing, fertility, purification, protection, money, returns hostility to sender, guilt, grief, regrets	Mars
Poison (Christian Dior)	N/A P, S	Includes: rose, cinnamon, carnation, jasmine, vetivert, musk, vanilla		N/A
Poppy	*Papaver somniferum* F, I, H	Coughs/bronchial disorders, insomnia, throat problems	Fertility, sleep, money, luck, invisibility in a threatening situation	Moon
Prelude (Balenciaga)	N/A P, S	Includes: bergamot, orange, carnation, jasmine, rose, ylang ylang, cinnamon, vanilla		N/A
Quartz (Molyneux)	N/A P, S	Includes: hyacinth, jasmine, rose, carnation, musk		N/A
Quelques Fleurs L'Original (Houbigant)	N/A P, S	Includes: bergamot, lemon, rose, jasmine, lily of the valley, carnation, ylang ylang, musk		N/A
Rose	*Rosa damascena* F, H, O, I, Sm, soul fragrance	Anger/irritability, high blood pressure, burns, poor circulation, insomnia, liver/gall bladder problems, menopausal problems, absent/painful menstruation, panic/ phobias, skin allergies/ rashes, stress	Love and love divination, enchantment, psychic development, healing, luck, protection, heals abuse especially from childhood, guilt, grief, regrets	Venus
Rosemary	*Rosmarinus officinalis* H, I, O, Sm	Arthritis/rheumatism, burns, poor circulation, exhaustion, headaches/ migraines, liver/gall bladder problems, absent/painful menstruation, PMT, skin allergies/rashes	Love, passion, increases mental powers, removes negativity and depression, banishes nightmares, purification, healing, quiet sleep	Sun

Fragrance	Latin name and form	Healing properties	Magical properties	Planet
Rosewood	*Aniba rosaeodora* O, I, H	Stress, insomnia, skin problems, scar tissue, wounds/operations	Peace, reconciliation, quiet happiness, healing of old sorrows	Venus
Safari (Ralph Lauren) P, S	N/A	Includes: orange, jasmine		N/A
Saffron	*Carthamus tinctorius* F, H, O, spice	Painful or delayed menstruation, digestive disorders	Love, lust, healing, happiness, raising the winds, passion, strength, psychic development, second sight	Sun
Sage	*Salvia officinalis* H, I, O	Anxiety, asthma, headaches/migraines, throat problems, exhaustion, lack of concentration	Long life, wisdom, protection, grants wishes, improves memory, good health, power, leadership, success	Jupiter
Sagebrush	*Artemisia* Sm	as above	as above	Jupiter
Sandalwood	*Santalum album* H, O, I, soul fragrance	Stress, sexual dysfunction, skin problems	Protection, healing, banishes negativity, spirituality, contact with guardian angels/higher self	Moon
Sweet marjoram	*Origanum majorana* H, O	Arthritis/rheumatism, asthma, insomnia	Protection, love, happiness, health, money, guilt, grief, regrets	Mercury
Sweetgrass	*Hierochloe odorata* H, Sm	Not used medicinally	Mother goddess, healing of abuse, old sorrows, gentleness, patience in nurturing others, calling spirits	Moon
Tea Tree	*Melaleuca alternifolia* H, I, O	Fungal infections, parasites, viruses, wounds	Cleansing, cuts through illusion, honesty, legal matters	Moon
Thyme	*Thymus vulgaris* H, I, O, Sm	Anxiety, poor circulation, colds/influenza, coughs/bronchitis/lung problems, throat problems, toothache/mouth problems, wounds/operations	Health, healing, prophetic dreams, psychic development, improves memory, love and love divination, purification, courage	Venus
Valerian	*Valeriana officinalis* H, O	Stress, anxiety, panic attacks, insomnia	Love and love divination, quiet sleep, fertility, purification, protection against hostility, inner fears and despair	Venus
Vanilla	*Vanilla aromatica* H, O, I	Digestion, skin problems, anxiety	Love, passion, increases mental acuity, fidelity, harmony	Venus

Fragrance	Latin name and form	Healing properties	Magical properties	Planet
Vetivert	*Vetiveria zizanoides* H, O, I	Depression, anxiety, arthritis, skin problems	Love, breaking a run of bad luck, money, anti-theft, protects against all negativity	Venus
Violet	*Viola odorata* F, I, O, soul fragrance	Colds/influenza, coughs/bronchitis/ lung problems, skin allergies/rashes, pain relief	Modesty, secrecy, uncovering hidden talents, new love, love that cannot be revealed	Venus
Ylang ylang	*Cananga odorata* F, O, I, soul fragrance	Tension, hair/skin problems	Love, passion, sensuality, self-esteem	Venus

Prohibitions

If you suffer from any chronic or potentially serious medical condition or have allergies or asthma, check with a pharmacist or qualified herbalist before using any herbs or oils.

The following herbs and oils should be avoided during pregnancy
Aloe vera, angelica, autumn crocus, barberry, basil, caraway, cayenne, cedarwood, clary sage, fennel, feverfew, goldenseal, hyssop, juniper, male fern, mandrake, marjoram, myrrh, parsley, pennyroyal, poke root, rosemary, rue, sage, southernwood, tansy, tarragon, thuja, thyme, wintergreen, wormwood and yarrow.

This is not a comprehensive list, so, as with any substance you use in pregnancy (especially in the early months), check with a herbalist or pharmacist first.

The following herbs and oils should be avoided if you are epileptic
Aniseed, camphor, fennel, hyssop, rosemary, sage and star anise.

The following herbs and oils should be avoided if you are on HRT
Clary sage, coriander (cilantro), fennel and Spanish sage.

Photo-toxic oils
These oils can irritate the skin if they are exposed to light. Use about half the usual amount and avoid direct sunlight for six hours after use: bergamot, ginger, lemon, lime, mandarin and orange.

Useful Reading

Angels
Davidson, Gustave, *A Dictionary of Angels*, Free Press, 1971
Ravenwolf, Silver, *Angels, Companions in Magick*, Llewellyn, 2001

Auras, chakras and colour therapy
Brennan, Barbara Anne, *Hands of Light: A Guide to Healing through the Human Energy Field*, Bantam Books, 1987
Eason, Cassandra, *Aura Reading*, Piatkus, 2000
Eason, Cassandra, *Chakra Power*, Quantum, 2001
Wauters, Ambika, *Homeopathic Color Remedies*, Crossing Press, 1999

Aromatherapy
Radford, Joan, *Family Aromatherapy*, Foulsham, 1999
Worwood, Valerie Ann, *The Fragrant Heavens*, Doubleday, 1999
Worwood, Valerie Ann, *The Fragrant Mind*, Doubleday, 1995

Candles
Bruce, Marie, *Candleburning Rituals*, Quantum, 2001
Buckland, Ray, *Advanced Candle Magic*, Llewellyn, 1996
Innes, Miranda, *The Book of Candles*, Dorling Kindersley, 1991

Flowers and plants
Chiazzari, Suzy, *Flower Readings*, CW Daniels Co, 2000
Tompkins, Peter and Christopher Bird, *Secret Life of Plants*, Avon Books, 1974
Vickery, Roy, *A Dictionary of Plant Lore*, Oxford University Press, 1995

General books on making fragrances, etc.
Groom, Nigel, *The Perfume Handbook*, Chapman & Hall, 1992
Reno, Kelly, *Good Gifts from the Home: Oils, Lotions and Other Luxuries Make Beautiful Gifts to Give*, Prima Publishing, 2002 (includes an A–Z of perfumes plus recipes)

Herbs
Bonar, Ann, *Herbs: A Complete Guide to their Cultivation and Use*, Tiger Books International, 1992
Cruden, Loren, *Medicine Grove: A Shamanic Herbal*, Inner Traditions, 1997
Culpeper, Nicholas, *Culpeper's Colour Herbal*, Foulsham, 2003
Culpeper, Nicholas, *Complete Herbal*, Bloomsbury Books, 1992
Cunningham, Scott, *Encyclopedia of Magical Herbs*, Llewellyn, 1997
Mabey, Richard, *The Complete New Herbal*, Penguin, 1991

Incense and smudging
Cunningham, Scott, *Complete Book of Incense, Oils and Brews*, Llewellyn, 1993
Eason, Cassandra, *Smudging and Incense Burning*, Quantum, 2001
Kavasch, Barrie E and Karen Baar, *American Indian Healing Arts: Herbs, Rituals and Remedies for Every Season of Life*, Thorsons, 2000

Magic and ritual
Bruce, Marie, *Everyday Spells for a Teenage Witch*, Quantum, 2002
Bruce, Marie, *The Witch's Almanac*, Quantum, 2003
Cunningham, Scott, *The Magical Household*, Llewellyn, 1995
Eason, Cassandra, *A Practical Guide to Witchcraft and Magic Spells*, Quantum, 2001
Eason, Cassandra, *Every Woman a Witch*, Quantum, 1996
Eason, Cassandra, *Everyday Spells for a Happy Life*, Foulsham, 2003

Psychic powers
Eason, Cassandra, *Ten Steps to Psychic Power*, Piatkus, 2002
Telasco, Patricia, *Shamanism in a 9 to 5 World*, Crossing Press, 2000

Useful Contacts

Most companies will supply by mail order over the internet. Where phone or e-mail details are not given, they are not provided by the firm.

Aromatherapy oils

Australia
Sunspirit Essential Oils
PO Box 85
Byron Bay
New South Wales 2481
Tel: 612 6685 6333
Website: sunspirit.com.au

UK
Shirley Price Aromatherapy
Essentia House
Upper Bond Street
Hinckley
Leicestershire
LE10 1RS
Tel: 01455 615466
Website:
www.shirleyprice.co.uk

US
Aroma for Life
Hoffman Consulting LCC
2316 Somerset Drive
New Orleans, LA 70131
Tel: 504 392 2862
Website:
www.aromaforlife.com

Fragrances, fragrant crafts, pot pourri, etc.

Australia
Auroma
39 Melverton Drive
Hallam
Victoria 3803
Tel: 03 9796 4833
E-mail:
auroma@ozemail.com.au

UK
Buttermilk Barn,
Homespun Americana Ltd
36 Garfield Street
Watford
Hertfordshire
WD24 5HB
Tel: 01923 447972
E mail:
Karen@ButtermilkBarn.com

US
Caswell and Massey Co., Ltd.
Mail-Order Division
111 8th Ave
New York, NY 10011
Tel: 212 620 0900

A World of Plenty
PO Box 1153
Duluth, MN55810
Website: www.worldof
plenty.com

Herbs and spices

Australia
Global Herb Supplies
Corner of Byrnes and Eccles
Street
Cairns
Mareeba
Queensland 4880
Tel: 617 4092 2882
E mail:
health@globalherbalsupplies.c
om
(dried herbs)

Canada
Chris and Claudia Sutton
Forget-me-Not Herbs 'n'
Wildflowers
R.R. #2, 1920 Beach Road
Oxford Mills,
ON KOG 1SO
Tel: 613 258 1246
E
mail:forgetmenot@achilles.net

Plants

UK
Herb Mail Order Service
Haelan Centre
42 The Broadway
London
N8 9DT
Tel: 020 8340 4258
Website: www.haelan.co.uk
(dried herbs and spices)

US
Lingle's Herbs
2055 North Lomina Avenue
Long Beach, CA 901815
Tel: 800 708 0633
E mail:info@linglesherbs.com

Herbal bath products, etc.

Australia
Earth, Water, Fire
PO Box 3107
Bracken Ridge
Queensland 4017
Tel: 617 805 3107
E mail:
info@earthwaterfire.com.au

UK
Moonthistle,
8 Alma Street,
Falkirk,
Central Region,
FK2 7HB
Tel: 07732 397978
Website:
www.moonthistle.co.uk

US
Herbal Allies,
63 Clove Road
Wantage, NJ 07461
Tel: 973 702 3451
E-mail:
info@herbalalliesinc.com
(also dream pillows)

Smudging equipment, smudge sticks, smudge herbs, incenses, tools, etc.

Australia
Eartharomas Earthcraft
Magpie Flats Herb Farm
273/295 Boyle Road
Kenilworth
Queensland 4574
Website:
www.eartharomas.com.au

UK
Dreamcatcher Trading
118 Murray Road
Sheffield,
South Yorkshire
S11 7GH
Tel: 0114 268 7654
Website:
info@dreamcatchertrading.co
m

New Moon Occult Shop
PO Box 110
Didcot
Oxon
OX11 9YT
Tel: 01235 819744
E-mail: sales@new-
moon.demon.co.uk

US
Arizona Gateway Trading Post
Mail-HC 37,
Box 919-UPS 14265
N. Hiway 93
Golden Valley, AZ 86413
Tel: 928 767 4702
E-mail: agtp@citlink.net

Tibetan Incense Company
53 South 200 East
Kanab
Utah, 84741
Tel: 435 874 9644
E-mail:
Russell@tibetanincense.com

Spiritual healing

Australia
Australian Spiritualist
Association,
PO Box 248
Canterbury,
New South Wales 2193

Canada
Association of Spiritual Healers
of Alberta
7535 Hunterview Drive NW
Calgary
Alberta
T2K 4P7
Contact: Mrs Betty Peterson
(Chair)
E-mail:
edbetty@telusplanet.net

Healing Network International
(Ontario Chapter)
3504 / 85 Thorncliffe Park
Drive
Toronto
Ontario
M4H 1L4
Contact: Ms Merosia
Butschynski (1st Officer)
E-mail: albry@interlog.com

New Zealand
National Federation of Spiritual
Healers
PO Box 764
Thames,
New Zealand
Contact: Bob & Jan Arnold
E-mail: bob.jan@xtra.co.nz
Web: www.nfsh.org.nz

UK
British Alliance of Healing
Associations
Mrs Jo Wallace
3 Sandy Lane
Gisleham
Lowestoft
Suffolk
NR 33 8EQ

National Federation of Spiritual
Healers
Old Manor Farm Studio
Church Street
Sunbury on Thames
Middlesex
TW16 6RG

US
Heart Awakening Project Inc
PO Box 4195
Cave Creek, AS 85327
Contact: Mr Raout Bertrand
(President)
E-mail:
service@heartawakening.com
Web: www.heartawakening.com

Index

acacia 93, 107, 122, 125, 151
Air *see* elements
allspice 107, 126, 145
almond 53, 121, 125–6, 145, 151
altar making and empowerment 16–17,
138–9
ambergris 12, 68
angelic communication and prayer 104–19
angelica 82, 125, 180
correspondences 171
magical properties 145
angels and archangels 109–19, 128–6, 137
anise 82, 123, 126–7
apple trees and blossom 85, 96, 110, 126,
141
association with Taurus 121
for healing 151, 155
magical properties 145
apricot 151
Aquarius 122, 127
Aries 120–1, 126
aromatic oils 90–1
artificial fragrances 12
astral travel 98–100
astrology and divination 120–36
aura reading for chakra problems 70–1
automatic writing 134–5
autumn crocus 180

basil 53, 99, 126, 140, 180
association with Scorpio 122
correspondences 171
for healing 151, 155, 156
magical properties 145
bath fragrances 74, 75–82
bay 49–50, 52, 59, 106, 125, 141
association with Leo 121
correspondences 171
for healing 151, 156
magical properties 145
benzoin 107, 122, 125, 145
bergamot 52, 53, 180
correspondences 172
for healing 151, 155, 156
magical properties 145

Cancer 121, 125
candles 13, 28
for the chakras 74
for peaceful sleep 85
unlocking psychic senses 91–2

Capricorn 122, 127
carnation 53, 78, 93, 94, 99, 110, 125
angel 111
association with Aries 120–1
correspondences 172
magical properties 145
carrier oils 13
catnip 50, 78, 145
cedar 107, 145
cedarwood 93, 96, 99, 101, 103, 126–7,
180
correspondences 172
chakra system 62–74, 165–9
chamomile 51–2, 59, 78, 82, 85, 106, 125
association with Taurus 121
correspondences 172
for healing 151, 155, 156
magical properties 145
cherry trees and blossom 122, 126, 145,
151
cinnamon 106, 107
correspondences 172
magical properties 145
citronella 52, 172
citrus fragrances 44, 82
clairsentience 20–3
clary sage 82, 180
correspondences 172
for healing 151, 155, 156
clove 82, 107, 126–7, 145, 172
coconut 96, 125, 145, 151
commercial perfumes *see* Fragrant
Correspondences 171–80
copal 99, 101, 107, 125
coriander (cilantro) 126, 145, 180
crystal and stone divination 128, 158
cypress 101, 121, 126, 127

dill 50, 125–6
association with Gemini 121
correspondences 172
for healing 151, 156
magical properties 145
divination
and astrology 120–36, 127–8
automatic writing 134–5
dragon's blood 126, 146
dreams 75–87

Earth *see* elements
echinacea 126

elderflower 78, 172
elements 17–18, 53
  elemental empowerment 29–31, 141
environmental healing 153
epilepsy 180
essential oils 12–13, 41, 51, 59, 92
eucalyptus 52, 59, 78, 125
  association with Cancer 121
  correspondences 172

fennel 59, 78, 125–6, 180
  Archangel Raphael 131–2
  association with Virgo 121
  correspondences 174
  for healing 151, 155, 156
  magical properties 146
fern 53, 92, 146, 174, 180
feverfew 126, 180
Fire see elements
floral fragrances 110, 43–4
flower waters 35–8, 92
flowers 73, 144–8
fragrance
  angels 109–17
  for clairsentience 21–2
  how it works 4–5
  making your own 34–41
  meditation 94–6
  and personality type 43–8
  and personal prayer 104–9
  visualisation 96–8
fragrant store cupboard 11–15
frankincense 66, 83, 107, 125
  Archangel Michael 130
  association with Leo 121
  correspondences 174
  spiritual development 89, 92, 94, 96,
    99, 101
freesia 146

gardenia 121, 125
gardens 56–8, 150–1
garlic 51, 57
Gemini 121, 125–6
geranium 53, 110, 126
  angel 111–12
  association with Scorpio 122
  correspondences 174
  for healing 151, 155, 156
  magical properties 146
ginger 122, 126, 146, 180

healing with fragrance 90, 149–159
heather 53, 146, 174
heliotrope 18
herbaceous fragrances 44

herbs
  magical properties 144–8
  storing 14
hibiscus 53, 96, 99, 101, 110, 126
  angel 112
  association with Sagittarius 122
  correspondences 174
  magical properties 146
  personal prayer 106, 107
home
  fragrant protection 10–11, 49–58
honeysuckle 50, 53, 110, 126–7
  angel 112
  association with Aries 120–1
  correspondences 174
  magical properties 146
hops 78, 82
hyacinth 53, 93, 101, 110, 126, 127
  angel 113
  association with Capricorn 122
  correspondences 174
  for healing 151, 155
  magical properties 146
hydrangea 122
hyssop 78, 180

incense 12, 90, 93, 106–9
indoor fragrant place 15–16
infused and essential oils 38–41
ivy 92, 146
jasmine 51–2, 53, 65, 92, 110, 125
  angel 113
  Archangel Gabriel 130
  association with Cancer 121
  correspondences 174
  dreams 78, 85
  for healing 151, 155, 156
  magical properties 146
  spiritual development 92, 93, 94, 101

jojoba 13
journal of fragrance blends 15
juniper 103, 106–7, 107, 125, 180
  correspondences 175
  for healing 151, 155, 156
  magical properties 146
Jupiter 126–7, 132–3

lavender 50, 59, 67, 69, 106, 110, 125–6
  angel 113–14
  Archangel Raphael 131–2
  association with Gemini and Virgo 121
  correspondences 175
  dreams 78, 82, 85
  for healing 151, 155, 156
  magical properties 146
  spiritual development 92, 93, 94, 101

leaf fragrances 44–5
lemon 53, 125, 180
  association with Pisces 123
  correspondences 175
  for healing 151, 155, 156
  magical properties 146
lemon balm *see* melissa
lemon verbena 53, 59, 78, 127
  association with Cancer 121
  correspondences 175
  for healing 151, 155
  magical properties 146
lemongrass 52, 96, 125–6
  association with Gemini 121
  correspondences 175
  magical properties 146
Leo 121, 125
Libra 122, 126
lilac 50, 78, 83, 101, 110, 126
  angel 114
  association with Taurus 121
  correspondences 175
  magical properties 146
lily 110, 126
  angel 114
  association with Virgo 121
  correspondences 176
  magical properties 146
  symbol of love 160
lily of the valley 125–6
  association with Gemini 121
  correspondences 176
  for healing 151, 155
  magical properties 147
lime 122, 125, 176, 180
linden blossom 78, 110, 115, 126–7, 176
lotus 68, 69, 89, 101, 110, 125
  angel 115
  association with Pisces 123
  correspondences 176
  magical properties 147
love and fragrance 160–9

magical properties of herbs, flowers and
  trees 144–8
magnolia 122, 126
mandarin 180
marigold 53, 125
  association with Leo 121
  correspondences 176
  for healing 151, 155, 156
  magical properties 147
marjoram 53, 122, 180
  see also sweet marjoram
Mars 126, 131
meadowsweet 126–7, 147, 151, 155,
  156, 176

meditation 90, 91, 93–6
melissa 51–2, 78, 94, 125, 155
  association with Cancer 121
  for healing 151, 155, 156
  magical properties 147
menopause and HRT 156, 180
Mercury 125–6, 131–2
mimosa 53, 65, 82, 85, 94, 101, 110, 127
  angel 115–16
  Archangel Cassiel 133–4
  association with Scorpio 122
  correspondences 176
  magical properties 147
mint 99, 126, 140, 176
modifying your personality mix 47–8
moon 125, 130
  phases 34, 140, 153, 163
mullein 83
musk 12, 94, 123, 177
myrrh 83, 89, 92, 94, 101, 107, 125, 180
  Archangel Gabriel 130
  association with Capricorn 122
  correspondences 177
  magical properties 147
myrtle 45

neroli *see* orange blossom
nettles 50
nutmeg 126–7

oakmoss 17
olive and olive blossom 78, 151, 156
orange 59, 94, 96, 125, 180
  Archangel Michael 130
  association with Leo 121
  correspondences 177
  dreams 76, 78, 82, 83
  for healing 151, 155, 156
  magical properties 147
orange blossom 51–2, 53, 59, 78, 110
  angel 116
  association with Sagittarius 122
  correspondences 177
  symbol of love and fertility 160
orchid 122
outdoor fragrant place 19–20, 57–8

pansy 127
papyrus flower 68, 69, 101, 177
parsley 125–6, 180
  correspondences 177
  for healing 151, 156
  magical properties 147
passionflower 78, 126
  correspondences 177
  for healing 151, 155, 156
  magical properties 147

past-life recall 100–3
patchouli 127, 141
    Archangel Cassiel 133–4
    association with Virgo 121
    correspondences 177
peach 53, 76, 96, 126
    association with Libra 122
    for healing 151
pendulum dowsing 48, 69–70, 93, 128,
    153, 159
pennyroyal 147, 180
peppermint 52, 53, 78, 82, 83, 123
    Archangel Camiel 131
    association with Aries 120–1
    correspondences 178
    for healing 151, 155, 156
    magical properties 147
personal power oils 41–8
personality type and fragrance 43–8
pine 59, 99, 101, 106, 107, 126, 141
    Archangel Camiel 131
    association with Aries 120–1
    correspondences 178
    for healing 151, 155
    home protection 52, 53
    magical properties 147
Pisces 123, 126–7
planetary fragrances 124–7
plant psychometry and healing 157–9
poppy 125, 147, 178
pot pourri 14, 52–6
prayer and angelic communication 104–19
pregnancy 69, 161, 180
prohibitions 180
psychic powers and senses 20–3, 90–2

recipes
    bath fragrances 79–82
    dream pillow 83–5
    flower waters 35–8
    infused and essential oils 38–41, 47, 51
    to modify your personality mix 47–8
    pot pourri 53–6
    perfumed unguent 40
rituals and spells
    altar purification and
        empowerment 138–9
    archangel divination 134–6
    basic spell-casting 143–4
    bath rituals 76–7, 79–82
    to bury illness and grow better
        health 151–5
    candlelight empowerment 28
    for the chakras 71–4, 164–9
    to contact your personal angel 118–19
    elemental rituals 29–31, 41–3
    empowering bought flower waters 38

five stages of fragrance spells 140-8
fragrance meditation 94–6
fragrance visualisation 97–8
full moon empowerment 28–9
to identify your fragrance angel 117–18
to induce astral travel 99–100
to induce dreams 86, 87
incense for prayer and ritual 107–9
love spells 164–9
past-life exploration 101–3
plant psychometry 158–9
to release fear 136
signature fragrance empowerment 27–31
to smoke out bad vibes 60–1
white flower empowerment ritual 29
root fragrances 45
rose 50, 59, 67, 92, 93, 101, 110, 126, 140
    angel 116
    Archangel Anael 133
    association with Taurus 121
    correspondences 178
    dreams 76, 78, 82, 83, 85
    for healing 151, 155, 156
    magical properties 147
    symbol of love 160, 161–4
rose water 36–7, 69
rosemary 78, 83, 99, 106, 125–6,180
    association with Aquarius 122
    correspondences 178
    for healing 151, 155, 156
    home protection 51, 53
    magical properties 147
rosewood 52, 82, 93, 94, 99, 126
    association with Capricorn 122
    correspondences 179
    for healing 156

Safari 179
saffron 125, 148, 179
sage 51, 74, 99, 101, 126–7, 140, 180
    Archangel Sachiel 132–3
association with Sagittarius 122
    correspondences 179
    for healing 151, 155, 156
    magical properties 148
    prayer 106, 107
    workplace protection 59, 60
sagebrush 60, 74, 148, 179
Sagittarius 122, 126–7
St John's wort 83, 125, 161
    for healing 151, 155, 156
    magical properties 148
sandalwood 53, 106, 107, 126–7
    Archangel Sachiel 132–3
    association with Scorpio 122
    correspondences 179
    dreams 82, 83, 85

magical properties 148
past-life recall 101, 103
spiritual development 89, 92, 93, 94,
    96, 99
Saturn 127, 133–4
Scorpio 122, 126
signature fragrance 14, 93, 110
    empowering 27–32
    identifying 25–6
skullcap 79
slippery elm 79
smudging 13, 60–1, 74, 109
soul fragrance identifying 92–3
spearmint 148
spells *see* rituals and spells
spice fragrances 45
spiritual development 88–103
strawberry 96, 126
sun 34, 125, 129–30
sun sign fragrances 120–4
sunflower 121
sweet almond 13
sweet fragrances 45–6
sweet marjoram 78, 83, 94, 99, 101, 127
    correspondences 179
    for healing 155
    magical properties 148
sweet pea 123, 141, 148
sweetgrass 123, 148, 179

tangerine 125
tarragon 126, 180
Taurus 121, 126
tea tree 59, 125, 179
therapeutic plants 149–50
thyme 52, 59, 99, 101, 106, 107, 123,
    126, 180

association with Aries 120–1
    correspondences 179
    for healing 151, 155, 156
    magical properties 148
turmeric 45

valerian 79, 83, 125–6
    correspondences 179
    magical properties 148
vanilla 53, 96, 126
    Archangel Anael 133
    association with Libra 122
    correspondences 179
    magical properties 148
Venus 126, 133
vervain 121, 126
vetivert 127
    association with Capricorn 122
    correspondences 180
    magical properties 148
violet 53, 110
    angel 117
    correspondences 180
    for healing 151, 155, 156
    magical properties 148
Virgo 121, 125–6
visualisation 90, 91, 96–8

Water *see* elements
woody fragrances 46
workplace protection 58–61

yerba santa 148
ylang ylang 51–2, 76, 83, 85, 94, 126, 148
    association with Libra 122
    correspondences 180